THE
POWER of
AWAKENING

Also by Dr. Wayne W. Dyer

BOOKS

Being in Balance

Change Your Thoughts—Change Your Life

Don't Die with Your Music Still in You (with Serena J. Dyer)

Everyday Wisdom

Everyday Wisdom for Success

Excuses Begone!

Getting in the Gap

Good-bye, Bumps! (children's book with Saje Dyer)

Happiness Is the Way

I Am (children's book with Kristina Tracy)

I Can See Clearly Now

Incredible You! (children's book with Kristina Tracy)

The Invisible Force

It's Not What You've Got! (children's book with Kristina Tracy)

Living an Inspired Life

Living the Wisdom of the Tao

Memories of Heaven

My Greatest Teacher (with Lynn Lauber)

No Excuses! (children's book with Kristina Tracy)

The Power of Intention

The Power of Intention (gift edition)

A Promise Is a Promise

The Shift

Staying on the Path

10 Secrets for Success and Inner Peace

Unstoppable Me! (children's book with Kristina Tracy)

You Are What You Think

Your Ultimate Calling

Wishes Fulfilled

AUDIO/CD PROGRAMS

Advancing Your Spirit (with Marianne Williamson)

Applying the 10 Secrets for Success and Inner Peace

The Caroline Myss & Wayne Dyer Seminar

Change Your Thoughts—Change Your Life (unabridged audiobook)

Change Your Thoughts Meditation

Divine Love

Dr. Wayne W. Dyer Unplugged (interviews with Lisa Garr)

Everyday Wisdom (audiobook)

Excuses Begone! (available as an audiobook and a lecture)

How to Get What You Really, Really, Really, Really Want

I AM Wishes Fulfilled Meditation (with James Twyman)

I Can See Clearly Now (unabridged audiobook)

The Importance of Being Extraordinary (with Eckhart Tolle)

Inspiration (abridged 4-CD set)

Inspirational Thoughts

Making the Shift (6-CD set)

Making Your Thoughts Work for You (with Byron Katie)

Meditations for Manifesting

101 Ways to Transform Your Life
(audiobook)

The Power of Intention
(abridged 4-CD set)

A Promise Is a Promise (audiobook)

Secrets of Manifesting

The Secrets of the Power of Intention
(6-CD set)

10 Secrets for Success and Inner Peace

*There Is a Spiritual Solution to
Every Problem*

*The Wayne Dyer
Audio Collection/CD Collection*

Wishes Fulfilled
(unabridged audiobook)

DVDs

*Change Your Thoughts—
Change Your Life*

Excuses Begone!

Experiencing the Miraculous

I Can See Clearly Now

The Importance of Being Extraordinary
(with Eckhart Tolle)

Inspiration

*Modern Wisdom from the
Ancient World*

My Greatest Teacher (a film with bonus
material featuring Wayne Dyer)

The Power of Intention

The Shift, the movie (available as a
1-DVD program and an expanded
2-DVD set)

10 Secrets for Success and Inner Peace

*There's a Spiritual Solution to
Every Problem*

Wishes Fulfilled

MISCELLANEOUS

*Daily Inspiration from
Dr. Wayne W. Dyer Calendar*
(for each individual year)

The Essential Wayne Dyer Collection
(comprising *The Power of Intention,
Inspiration,* and *Excuses Begone!* in a
single volume)

The Shift Box Set
(includes *The Shift* DVD and
The Shift tradepaper book)

All of the above are available at your local bookstore, or may be ordered
by visiting: Hay House USA: www.hayhouse.com; Hay House Australia:
www.hayhouse.com.au; Hay House UK: www.hayhouse.co.uk;
Hay House India: www.hayhouse.co.in

Published in the United States by: Hay House, Inc.: www.hayhouse.com®
Published in Australia by: Hay House Australia Pty. Ltd.: www.hayhouse.com.au
Published in the United Kingdom by: Hay House UK, Ltd.: www.hayhouse.co.uk
Published in India by: Hay House Publishers India: www.hayhouse.co.in

Cover design: Scott Breidenthal • *Interior design:* Nick C. Welch

Material in this book originally appeared in the form of audiotapes of Wayne Dyer's lectures as *How to Be a No-Limit Person, Secrets of the Universe, Choosing Your Own Greatness, Transformation, The Awakened Life,* and *Freedom Through Higher Awareness* published by Nightingale-Conant.

The author of this book does not dispense medical advice or prescribe the use of any technique as a form of treatment for physical, emotional, or medical problems without the advice of a physician, either directly or indirectly. The intent of the author is only to offer information of a general nature to help you in your quest for emotional and spiritual well-being. In the event you use any of the information in this book for yourself, the author and the publisher assume no responsibility for your actions.

Cataloging-in-Publication Data is on file with the Library of Congress

Hardcover ISBN: 978-1-4019-5608-0
E-book ISBN: 978-1-4019-5610-3

10 9 8 7 6 5 4 3
1st edition, October 2020

Printed in the United States of America

THE POWER of AWAKENING

Mindfulness Practices and Spiritual Tools
to Transform Your Life

DR. WAYNE W.
DYER

HAY HOUSE, INC.
Carlsbad, California • New York City
London • Sydney • New Delhi

CONTENTS

FOREWORD

All of a sudden you start seeing miracles happening,
and it's absolutely astounding to you.

— Dr. Wayne W. Dyer

Fear has taken hold.
The world is in crisis.

It's late March 2020, and a global pandemic called coronavirus is spreading.

As I type these words, my wife, Denise, and I are on orders not to leave our home. Yet we are not alone: *Half* of all Americans have now been issued some kind of stay-at-home order. More will come. Globally, billions of people are facing and will continue to face government restrictions.

By the time you read this, perhaps you know how all this turns out. But it is all new to us.

Quarantines, social distancing, mass gathering cancellations, and *economic shutdowns* are words we are all just getting used to saying.

First, there were the warnings. A mysterious virus emerged in China. Then the inevitable confusion, avoidance, and denial. Then the contagion spread quickly beyond borders. Then mass panic. Then, in just weeks, no choice: travel restricted, schools closed, workers sent home, countries locked down all over the globe.

More news comes every day that shakes the foundation of our comforts and certainties. Hoarding of basic supplies, overwhelmed hospitals, increasing regulations, the vitriol of blame, the worldwide economy on the brink, and, every day in the headlines, rising infections and death, everywhere.

For much of the globe, there is this constant, grueling terror of the unknown. The kind that leads us to repeatedly ask *why* and *how* and *who* to blame and *what* now—impossible questions that lead to sleepless nights, endless speculation with friends, shifting social blame, political conspiracy, and the heart-wrenching reality of watching the death rate climb with exponential precision.

The economy in the United States has collapsed into recession, leading to a $2 trillion stimulus package, which many acknowledge will make barely a dent. Three million filed for unemployment last week. Tens of millions more are expected. Businesses, good ones, are shuttering everywhere. Countries continue to lock down. More restrictions are coming. There is no vaccine in sight.

And yet, mercifully, I type these words feeling *deeply at peace.* The emotional contagions of fear and scarcity have not pierced my mind, body, or spirit.

Somehow, I feel calm. Centered. Responsible for my emotions. Self-reliant in the face of infinite danger and spreading death. Removed from the need of grasping in hopes of controlling it all.

The shelves at my grocery store, before it closed, were empty of basic needs—and yet I feel abundance.

Like most of the world, I am likely to get infected at some point—and yet I feel safe, whole, complete.

I am locked in my house, but I am authentically and spiritually free.

Thousands of people message me every day. They are scared, seeking guidance and hope, and often demonstrating anger, terror, anxiety. And yet, I've not been pulled into the abyss. I feel a confidence that is hard to explain—ready to serve.

Optimism and faith blanket me. I observe my worried thoughts and the instant reactions, sensing an egocentric concern for self, and yet most of my day is asking, "How can I serve others now?"

I am finding appreciation and even moments of bliss in these seemingly dark days and nights. For this perspective and ability, I have Wayne Dyer to thank.

Oh, believe me, I'm not perfect and I'm not always brave. But I am here, fully here, centered and positive, thanks to Wayne's wisdom and influence throughout my life.

Wayne was, and still is, a vital part of my own awakening. Especially now.

THE DISTANT MENTOR

It's been 24 years since I read my first Wayne Dyer book. Though Wayne passed away five years ago, this book that you are holding is Wayne's 43rd. I can't think of a more important time for his message.

What's the promise of this book amid these chaotic times? In my view, it's what Wayne often taught:

> *There is a higher place that each of us can reach*
> *while we are here.*

And when you *awaken* to that potential, which is what this book is about, "you live according to your higher self, which promotes peace, fulfillment, integrity, and joy."

Note that Wayne didn't reference circumstance. You don't need a lucky break—you simply choose to *live according to your higher self,* and it just *happens.* Awakening isn't contingent upon convenience or ease. It can just happen, even now.

Somehow, I find comfort in that. My entire adult life, I've found solace and freedom in Wayne's message.

When I was 19 years old, I was suicidal. A breakup with my high school sweetheart sent me over the edge. She had cheated, and since my entire identity was wrapped up in our relationship, once the relationship ended so did my conception of self and purpose. Sometimes, when your relationship falls apart, you fall apart. That's what happened—I became *unraveled*, lost and depressed. I planned on taking my life, and I planned how and when to do it.

But then, as it happens, life had other plans. One night, I was in a car accident where the car rolled several times off a highway. I found myself pulling my body through the windshield to escape and standing on the crumpled hood of the car. Blood was running down my legs. Fear surged through my entire body.

And then, I felt faint. I thought I was going to die.

I looked down at all the blood spilling off my feet and onto the hood of the car. I thought this was it: *Did I even matter?* I felt my gaze pull to the sky and there was this great big beautiful moon. And in that *instant* I looked up, I felt freed of pain, suddenly safe. I spontaneously awoke to life's preciousness and magic. God had given me a second chance.

That sad and heartbroken and suicidal kid didn't want to die anymore. I wanted to *live*. I wanted to love again. I wanted to matter.

That night began my commitment to learning how to change and improve my life.

Fast-forward a few weeks, and after recovering, I started browsing bookstores for my existential questions. I found the self-improvement section and was drawn to an audiobook by Wayne Dyer.

In a serendipitous turn of events that I know Wayne would have loved, the first thing I consumed was his audio program *The Awakened Life*.

(When Hay House asked me to write the foreword to this book, I gleefully agreed without even knowing its title. I remember opening the manuscript and seeing *The Power of Awakening* and thought, *Full circle, my friend. Well done. Thank you.*)

Wayne's audio program *How to Be a No-Limit Person* and his book *Real Magic* were next, and essential to opening my mind in my 20s.

Years later, after the 9/11 terrorist attacks, I found comfort and hope in *There's a Spiritual Solution to Every Problem*.

What was I learning from Wayne?

That attitude matters. Intention matters. Love matters. Faith matters. Ego, control, materialism, and power over others do not. Serve others and you are serving a purpose. Tap into a higher consciousness and you access your highest self. You can be at peace and feel joy even amid what seems like chaos. Find stillness within. Look for miracles. Surrender can be strength. *Act in accordance with love, with the Divine.*

By 2003, these lessons were paying off. I was happy and in love. I felt good mentally, emotionally, and spiritually. I had manifested a good job as a leadership consultant. It was satisfying, challenging, and service-driven work.

But I felt called for something else. I wanted to be a writer.

I had visions of myself public speaking and talking about my books, like a young but less skilled, and definitively less wise, Wayne Dyer. It's not that I felt I could be like Wayne— it's that he was an example of what I viewed as a *career choice.* I didn't want to follow or mimic him; I wanted a career like his, helping people. I felt called to that.

Wayne taught that most of us don't allow ourselves the freedom to listen to those internal callings. I decided to listen to my dreams because, no doubt, somewhere in the recesses of my mind, Wayne had influenced me to do so.

I wrote my first book, *Life's Golden Ticket*, with great hope. I poured everything into it. It was the artistic achievement of my lifetime. I couldn't wait to share it with the world. Slowly, though, over many months, 19 publishers rejected it. I was crushed and ready to return to my safe corporate job. I considered quitting on my dream.

Then I read *Your Sacred Self.*

Months later, *The Power of Intention.*

There was no going back now.

Wayne's teachings helped crystallize my purpose and fuel my desire for what he calls in this book *authentic freedom.*

I went broke in my quest to find a publisher and become a speaker. Eventually, I found a publisher. We launched the book, and it failed their expectations. But I had intention— I was going to succeed at this career.

So I decided to double down and do whatever it took to manifest my dreams (something Wayne teaches in this book). I surrendered the need to have others recognize my work, and I started learning to be a better writer; to do marketing better; to start a business; to live a fuller, freer life.

I learned not to force it, even though I had a lot of vision and hope and intention. It's like Wayne often taught in his PBS specials, life is a dream and you are blessed to row, row, row *your* boat, gently down the stream . . . merrily. . . .

Within a few short years, I was at ease in the stream of life and wrote another book. It became a #1 *New York Times* bestseller. Suddenly, I was speaking all over the country and coaching influential people. Life was becoming the dream . . . I had my dream career as a writer, speaker, and coach.

It was as Wayne said it would be—when you trust and set intentions and seek your goals with flow and faith, "all of a sudden you start seeing miracles happening, and it's absolutely astounding to you."

In 2010, it came full circle. I had invited Wayne to speak at one of my seminars, and he accepted. We met for the first time, backstage at my event, just minutes before I went onstage and explained to my audience the difference he had made in my life. I was so giddy . . . "all of a sudden . . . miracles . . . it's absolutely astounding to you."

I watched Wayne awaken my audience to miracles, to God, to life, to love.

After he finished his talk, Wayne was so gracious to me and my team and everyone backstage. Before he left, he gave me the impression we'd see each other again soon.

"HOW THINGS UNFOLD"

A year later, Reid Tracy, CEO of Hay House, invited me to join Wayne's group tour to three sacred spiritual sites in Europe. I said yes. It was an honor to be anywhere near Wayne, and, secretly, I was having a difficult time in my life and wasn't aware of precisely why.

The itinerary was to take Wayne's fans and family to Assisi in Italy, Lourdes in France, and Medjugorje in Bosnia-Herzegovina. These were locations of famous spiritual sightings and miracles. At each stop, Wayne would share the location's history with us and how we might find our own spiritual path and miracles in life.

I have fond memories of Wayne on that trip, which I want to share here. I think these little scenes into his life reveal a little about who he was. (I won't recount the entire trip here, just three personal moments that meant something to me. You can watch the trip on Hay House's program called *Experiencing the Miraculous: A Spiritual Journey to Assisi, Lourdes, and Medjugorje*.)

The first memory I have is from the day we arrived in Italy together. I remember going to the airport baggage area and waiting for my luggage to appear. There was Wayne, waiting for his bags with all of us. Keep in mind there were 80-some people on this trip—fans—and Wayne was beyond famous at this stage in his life. Usually, someone in his position would have an assistant get the bags while he snuck out of the airport wearing shades and headed to a private undisclosed hotel in a private car.

But Wayne lived his message and waited for his bags like everyone else; he was humble and self-reliant. When we stepped outside and he saw his private car waiting, he asked to ride on the bus with everyone else. These might seem like small and insignificant details. But if you knew Wayne, you know these things mattered.

The second thing I remember is from a breakfast. Wayne ate with the entire group and was kind enough to let me sit with him. I was excited because I wanted to find out how I could give back to my mentor. I wanted to ask how I could be of service to his mission.

At that stage of my life, I was only six years and three books into my "thought leader" career. I was a newbie and had little to offer Wayne. My unique ability, though, was that I had figured out the online space sooner than most people in our industry, leading to millions of online students and fans in the span of a year. It had become a thing, and almost everyone I talked to would ask me to promote something for them online—it was a new constant in my life.

"So is there anything at all that I can do for you, Wayne? Something I can share or promote for you? I'd like to give back and thank you in some way."

Wayne smiled and looked at me, then his plate of eggs. "I'm good, Brendon. Let's just see how things unfold."

That is likely the best thing I've learned from Wayne—*trusting in how things unfold.*

To this day, Wayne is one of three people I've ever met in this industry who didn't ask me for something. I'll never forget that.

The third thing I remember from our European adventure is how Wayne doted on his children. He was so transparent in his lectures, spoken in their presence, about his journey as a father, husband, and human. To hear a "guru" share with a paying crowd that he wasn't always a good dad, that he was still evolving and exploring himself and the world, that he was still discovering the power of love, that he wasn't in control, and that he was actively and genuinely seeking to connect with his kids while he still had time—this is rare. This is beautiful. This is the spirit of it all.

I had only briefly met Wayne's kids on that trip, but on that same morning, chatting over eggs, I shared with him what I had observed and heard from them: they loved their father and they were proud of him. Sometimes, when Wayne heard something from you, his nod, the sparkle in his eyes, his silent knowing—without a word, he imbued the moment with soul.

SOMETHING IS WRONG

Earlier, I shared with you that I was having a difficult time in my life when I was invited on the trip with Wayne. I didn't know what was wrong exactly. I just felt off.

As we visited sites known for spiritual miracles, I was struck by a sense that something was truly wrong with me. I was trying to write my next book on that trip, and the words were not flowing. They weren't even coming to mind. I was exhausted at all times. We were on a trip of exploration, but I just wanted to stay in bed. I didn't feel myself.

I wish I could say that the trip had healed me, but it did not. However, it did force me to figure out what was going on. Because, for goodness' sake, *How can I be on a spiritual journey with Wayne Dyer and not feel incredible?*

It turned out that, during that trip, my brain was starting to swell. Months prior, I had wrecked a four-wheeler. It was a spectacular crash at 40 miles per hour. I thought I had gotten away pretty lucky—just a few broken bones, a thrown-out hip, a dislocated shoulder, a broken rib, and a snapped wrist that required full reconstruction. It was painful, but I felt lucky because the ATV had not landed on me, which would have likely killed or paralyzed me. It was like a *second* second chance.

When I received medical help, the doctors tended to the obvious but failed to ask if I had been knocked unconscious. They scanned my bones to see the breaks, but no one scanned my brain. I didn't even know that was needed.

And so it was near the time of my trip with Wayne that my brain apparently began swelling. I didn't know that— I just felt awful. Upon returning home from Europe, I sought medical attention. A doctor listened to my descriptions and asked if I had been knocked unconscious recently. I told him no at first, but then he asked if I had any other injuries lately. I remembered the ATV accident. He said, "Oh. Well, did anyone look at your brain after the wreck?"

After a brain scan, I was diagnosed with a traumatic brain injury. The doctor said I was experiencing post-concussion syndrome.

It would take two years of healing to feel myself again. During that time, I learned a lot about allowing and leaned into Wayne's teachings again. I watched *The Shift* four or five times.

Now that you know about my accident, I'd like to share a final memory from that trip with Wayne. During the tour, I still had a brace on my wrist from the ATV accident. One night, a bunch of us were hanging out in the hotel lobby when Louise Hay came down to say hello. It was the first and only time I met her. I was a huge fan of Louise's, and I knew of Wayne's work because of what she and Reid had built.

Louise walked up to me, noticed the brace on my wrist, and asked if she could bless it. She placed her hand on the brace and directed me to close my eyes. Then she said a silent prayer for me and did what Louise always did—she sent loving energy. I felt a relief in my wrist and a breath of fresh air enter my being. Her presence, even just for a few minutes, was healing. With that, she stood, wished me well, and walked away.

Later I found out Louise probably didn't even know who I was when we met. She just saw someone in pain and sought to heal. Like Wayne, she was always of service. The two of them shaped so much of my life.

Three years later, Wayne passed away in his sleep.

Two years after that, nearly to the day, Louise passed away.

Like all my mentors, I hope to carry on the values of those who have taught me and share their message with those I'm blessed to reach. I pray for the wisdom to honor them and serve others with such humility and humanity.

I feel Louise whispering now, "You really can heal your life."

And I see Wayne's blue eyes glisten as he nods and his smile widens: "There is a higher place that each of us can reach while we are here."

WHAT WOULD WAYNE SAY IN A CRISIS?

Now I sit here today, in the presence of distant mentors and memories, having just read *The Power of Awakening*. Reading this book was like a conversation with an old friend and mentor, a reminder of what is important and possible and beautiful in life.

This is such a relevant message for this moment. Indeed, the world has just been upended in a matter of weeks because of coronavirus, and with it our very notions of who we are, what we mean to one another, and what the future holds. We are in the process of the very redefining of our global experience, and that is unsettling and scary. Whatever people had planned at the beginning of 2020, a lot has changed real fast. It brings to mind what I often heard Wayne share from the stage: "If you want to make God laugh, tell him your plans."

And yet this crisis is truly an opportunity to plan a new life, to awaken to a higher vision and experience for ourselves. As Wayne says in the pages ahead, "What really happens here is that your personal identity changes. . . . Certain activities and events that formerly carried meaning and motivated you are also no longer important."

Could anything better describe this situation?

There are so many gems in the pages ahead that might offer a view into what Wayne would tell us in any time of hardship. So let's consider this moment but also expand into future challenges and life. I fear being so presumptuous, but I also feel that any book from Wayne can be applied to today's world, crisis or not, good times and bad, when you're youthful and when you are wise.

Perhaps during difficult times, Wayne would remind us that some people will "allow the circumstances of their lives to determine what their inner world is like, so they find themselves angry, hurt, depressed, sad, or fearful because of external events."

Others might awaken and experience things differently. They would not "see problems, difficulties, or obstacles in the same way. Instead, they are now viewed as energy shifts. [They] think, *I know that this problem is going to disperse, like problems always do. This is an opportunity for me to see what I'm made out of, if I can handle it.*"

Wayne might ask us to view the fears of the moment and affirm, "I am more than what bothers me. I am more than my troubles."

He might pose this:

"Can you learn to witness your life rather than identify with it?" Believe it or not, that's where bliss resides, where higher awareness resides, where authentic freedom resides.

Maybe Wayne would consider the fact that so many of us are stuck at home, and then suggest:

Take time to appreciate the beauty in your life. Take time to be contemplative. Take time to see that this is a magnificent universe. There is an intelligence to this whole thing, and everything you come across has something that you can appreciate in it. Rather than filling your inner world with criticism, skepticism, doubt, anguish, or pain, understand that you always have a choice. All your thoughts are things that you control. Once you take to heart the idea that what you think about is what expands, you can put your attention and energy on that which you appreciate rather than that which you think is not working well for you. Then you will see these heightened-awareness things manifesting for yourself.

I'd like to think that Wayne would remind us that it's best not to be up worrying at all hours and trying to control everything.

The ego says, "You must be concerned with everything." The higher self says, "If you surrender, serve, go with the flow, have an overriding spiritual objective, and know that you are here for a purpose, there will not be time for what offends you."

What should we remember during difficult times? Wayne might begin by reminding us to look at what is still good in this world:

When you allow the higher part of yourself to focus on what's right with the world instead of what's wrong, you become more productive. Releasing negativity from your life, and not allowing the ego or your self-absorption to get in the way, helps you feel more powerful, in control, and at peace.

But how?

What can I focus on specifically, Wayne?

Maybe he'd answer that we should not just focus on the drama at hand, or even what is good and what is here now, but also to look within and visualize the future. To have the courage to ask:

What do I want to expand in my life?

Imagine that—expanding emotionally and spiritually now versus shutting down.

Next, he might suggest we follow our bliss and help others, and that when we do, it all gets so much easier:

The great irony is that when we get focused on following our bliss and being in the service of others, all those things that we seek so desperately—the success, the achievement, the performance—seem to arrive in our life in great amounts.

But what happens when we get discouraged or feel alone?

Perhaps Wayne would see us holed up in our homes and suggest that it's a blessing to be reminded how much we need each other. *Everyone is connected and necessary.*

He'd say take care of others, because when "you are on target in your life, in the service of others, you'll understand the serenity that I'm talking about."

Of course, and again, one cannot imagine what Wayne would say about anything. We can only imagine he would be on purpose with what he felt was why he showed up on this planet and how he lived here:

That God force, or love force, is what I am about, what I'm here for. The more I find myself acting in accordance with the Divine, the more wonderful things happen to me.

All the things I do, from writing and speaking to the appearances I make in the media, are motivated by a genuine internal desire to bring about more stability and peace and harmony in the world for people in some way.

Personally, it seems that the reason I showed up on this planet has something to do with teaching self-reliance.

Yes, let us first be self-reliant by finding our own emotional center, peace, and harmony. How can we begin? Wayne might suggest meditation:

Meditation has helped me gain peacefulness, serenity, and energy. One of the things I've discovered in the process is that my purpose is to love and to serve and to give, and I must evaluate every behavior, action, and thought I have in those terms: Am I loving, serving, or giving? *I believe that all of us are actually here to give; we're not here to get. Meditation helps us tap into the Divine energy that shows us we are all here to serve each other and be in harmony.*

And what might Wayne advise both during and after this scary moment, months and years after this pandemic has passed, after the vaccine is found, after we've found our footing and we enter the inevitable next uncertainties of life? Maybe:

You must allow yourself to trust the Divine. Surrender and become unattached to how things come out, even though this can be very difficult.

You simply have to be: *Be at peace. Be at joy. Be at bliss.*

Who knows what Wayne would say to you, specifically? You can always pick up any of his books, which I hope you will continue to do, and find your own answers.

But don't worry: You don't need to have all the answers. Knowing the answers isn't the game. You simply need to awaken and *be who you are.*

As Wayne would say with a wink, this isn't a matter of self-help but of self-*realization.*

In writing these last paragraphs, I realize just how much I miss Wayne. Though we only met a few blessed times, I've known him every year of my adult life through his writings and programs.

And in writing this Foreword, I must share that I wanted to write Wayne's entire biography and tell you the timeline and broad impact of his life. Instead, knowing that a person's legacy is really carried on story by story, person by person, I thought I'd just share what he meant to me and what I learned from him. It's my small window into his world, but, oh, how I love these memories and how I appreciate the opportunity to do my small part in carrying his legacy forward.

I cannot wait for you to finish each and every page. I hope you'll share your own personal lessons and any experiences with Wayne to whomever you reach.

His voice will carry on through your awakening and sharing. But, oh, how I wish we could call him together now, to have him explain to us, here and now, just one more time, that we can experience life more easily, that we can awaken from the fear and ego and chaos of it all, that we can choose to access the Divine rather than the discord, that we can, truly, faithfully, row, row, row our boats, gently, intentionally, merrily, down this blessed stream.

Life is a dream once you awaken.

— Brendon Burchard,
author of *Life's Golden Ticket*, *The Motivation Manifesto*, and *High Performance Habits*

March 28, 2020

INTRODUCTION

Wayne Dyer was always a teacher. Even when he became a therapist and then a best-selling author, he loved to share things he learned with others. And he had an extraordinary way of taking high-level concepts and grounding them, making them seem relatable to everyone.

Wayne was constantly open to new ideas, and he explored a variety of topics throughout his prolific speaking and writing career. As we combed through hours upon hours of tapes from speeches and presentations he gave to many varied audiences over many years, we wondered whether we could find content for this book that modern audiences would be able to relate to.

To our delight, we were struck by the timelessness of his message. Certain passages seemed so relevant to current events, you might swear that he wrote them yesterday. We laughed at his still singular sense of humor and way with words. We also realized that Wayne returned to a few themes over and over again, which still resonate today. We thought it would be helpful to take those themes and weave them throughout this book: *There is more than the physical world of form. Much of life is an illusion. All of us have a higher self, which is who we truly are, and it is Divine. We create everything we need; we can even manifest miracles. There is no separation; we are all one. Love, peace, and harmony are what makes life worthwhile, not meaningless possessions that we can't ever actually have.*

In these pages, he will take you on a journey from awakening to higher awareness, and then ultimately to enlightenment. He'll offer you spiritual tools to transcend your current circumstances and old patterns, and instruct you in mindfulness practices such as visualization and meditation, ultimately helping you reach a higher con-sciousness and true fulfillment. In the process, you'll come to understand consciousness and the Divine plan in ways you might never have considered before, so that changing your life for the better seems natural—even inevitable.

It was so comforting to feel Wayne reaching through the years with his words, inspiring and guiding us through the stress and challenges of these tumultuous times. We hope this book helps you feel the same way, warming your heart and filling you with hope.

— the Hay House editorial staff

CHAPTER 1

CHART THE COURSE AHEAD

Unmuddling the metaphysical has long been a goal of mine—that is, to take some of the concepts that seem so fuzzy to many people and clear them up and make them available to everyone. Why should the most important things that human beings need to learn be unexplainable or shrouded in mystery?

Before we go any further, I ask that you commit to opening yourself up to the topics I'll be discussing in this book. If you are someone who has only been willing to experience that which you felt was safe and don't like to go outside of those limits—well, try not being that kind of person anymore. Instead, endeavor to be open to new experiences. Don't limit yourself to only what you feel you can be comfortable with.

Each one of us has the phenomenal capacity to be able to experience the entire range of human experience, and I want you to know that we can do so with ease. All it takes is getting out of that one percent of living life through our physical form, shifting our perspective to see each other beyond the packages that encase us. When we do so, we'll discover that there's something much grander available to us all.

I once wrote a book called *You'll See It When You Believe It*, and I wholeheartedly agree with that concept. If you only believe what you see, then you are limited to what is on the surface. But if you understand that you'll see it when you believe it, then you know that there's a special intelligence in the universe behind everything that has life in it. When you're looking beyond what everybody else sees, all of a sudden you start seeing miracles happening. It's absolutely astounding to you! You get to a point where you see that you are much more than the stuff that you can get hold of. You're more than this form and what it can detect with its physical senses. You understand that who you are is much bigger, much greater, much more *Divine* than that.

When you see that special intelligence, or that special love, in all life, you think in accepting, loving, and kind ways toward everything and everyone. Before long you're creating new kinds of relationships and new kinds of excitement out of that love, and you're making things happen that you never thought could happen before. And then you are *expecting* miracles, instead of being surprised by them. You become truly awake, and your whole life changes.

I have noticed such an evolution taking place in my own self. Things that were once absolutely unavailable to me, based on the consciousness I had at the time, are now readily there for me. I can have them anytime I want. I've tried to note some of the qualities or characteristics that happened to me, which you can expect to see in yourself as well. This is the course we will chart throughout the pages to come. The power of that awakening is what this book is about.

THE AWAKENING PROCESS

What a wonderful concept it is to be awakened. It's like when you go to sleep at night and you're dreaming—the only way you know you're dreaming is to wake up. Then you're in a completely different world, a completely different experience. We're talking about a similar thing here. During the awakening process, you'll be looking back on the "dream" you've been living so far.

How do you know that you're becoming awakened, and a higher consciousness is taking over in your life? Well, it seems that there are levels you go through, which have nothing to do with your age, your gender, your occupation, or anything outside of yourself.

First and foremost, you perceive things differently. You clearly see the foibles of human beings: You see how restricted people are because of ancient beliefs, all of these old rules that have been passed on from generation to generation, which are no longer valid but still clung to. You even see it in yourself, how you conduct yourself based upon rules that no longer apply, which somebody else tried to impose on you. You don't get angry about it, though. You don't judge it or feel attached to it; you just see it.

It's the most amazing thing, this new intelligence that you begin to develop. For example, it gives you a dramatic freedom because you no longer have to be right. You'll see other people having an opinion contrary to yours, and instead of trying to fight with them or get them to come into your camp, you tell yourself, *Well, this is where they are right now.* Again, there is no judgment; you simply see this.

You develop an unbelievable compassion for all life-forms, which can be almost overwhelming to you when you're starting the awakening process. You have a love for other beings akin to the love that you had for yourself when you were most happy, when you were a youngster. You even feel it for people who are supposed to be your enemies or competition—though you no longer think in those terms. You perceive a Divinity in every single soul out there, and you don't want anyone or anything to get hurt. This new compassion is a big part of the awakening process.

One day when I was walking on the beach, I noticed an older man teaching a young boy how to fish. The man had caught a fish, but it was too small. He was going to throw it back into the ocean, but his line got tangled in the process. So this fish was flopping around there on the beach, gasping for water, and the man was so preoccupied with his line being tangled that he completely forgot about it. He was working on the line and talking to the kid about it, and I was standing there wondering what he was going to do about this fish.

It seemed to me that if he behaved as if all life were precious, then the first thing he'd do would be to take the fish and remove the hook very gently, and throw the creature back in the water. But his preoccupation was with his line being tangled, until he finally seemed to remember, and said, "Okay, we'll throw this back." He let the fish suffer for about two minutes until he threw it back, and then it got washed right back up on the beach. Again, the man didn't notice, so I went over and picked it up. I took the little fish out into the water, about 20 yards or so, because it was still alive. Eventually, it got whatever it needed and darted away.

This kind of behavior is common when you start to awaken: you have compassion for everything, whether it's another human being or a fish. It doesn't necessarily mean that you won't eat animals, for example, but you may look for a more humane way to conduct yourself on the food chain. Your personal ethics change as you get into this awakening process, and you begin to have standards that didn't apply before.

One way I've seen my own ethics change is that I've let go of my old need to be right. My urge to let people know how they're wrong and to put them in their place has greatly diminished; now it's easy for me to bite my tongue. In fact, it's become very difficult for me to have an encounter with another human being in which they go away angry or upset.

Another characteristic or quality you'll find in yourself is a decreased attachment to people. In particular, you're no longer attached to those who would control you in any way. Yes, you have this tremendous compassion and new intelligence, where you begin to see things that were unclear to you at one time in your life, but you don't have a preoccupation with getting everybody on your side. If you have controlling relationships, you understand that they aren't necessary anymore, and you start moving away from them. You'll initially move away in your own mind, telling yourself, *No, I won't be controlled.* You might find this uncomfortable at first, but after a while you become very peaceful inside and just slide away from those relationships altogether.

One of the big keys to awakening is you now see yourself as a person with no labels. You don't have to define yourself by your job title, your marital status, or how much money you have . . . you don't define yourself at all. The old labels that you always placed on yourself—*I am a college graduate. I am a professional. I am a husband. I am a father. I am a man*— no longer apply. Instead, you recognize the formlessness that you are.

You also do not see problems, difficulties, or obstacles in the same way. Instead, they are now viewed as energy shifts. You think, *I know that this problem is going to disperse, like problems always do. This is an opportunity for me to see what I'm made out of, if I can handle it.*

During one trip, for instance, I couldn't find the key to my hotel room. There was a time I would have gotten myself so worked up over that, but now I see things like this as a test. I knew it would work out, and if I didn't find the key, I could always get another one. I worked through that thought, and it wasn't 20 seconds later that I found the key.

It just showed up. While this is a simple example, I've found that the more I practice these energy shifts, the more things like this happen.

The next thing you'll notice about awakening is something I like to call "in an instant." That is, you now understand that which had once been clouded and mysterious to you in one instant. It's almost like now that you are more open, that openness allows you to experience things that you never experienced before.

For example, I can remember reading a classic book from India a few years ago and getting nothing out of it. But then I picked it up again the other day, and in an instant it all made absolute, total, perfect sense to me. I also used to avoid the parts of bookstores devoted to philosophy, or anything that even smacked of spiritualism or metaphysics or the like. I'd think, *Come on! If you can't see or get hold of it, it doesn't exist. That's all there is to it.* Then I began to find myself in those very sections, buying four or five books at a time, and underlining passages once I got them home. It's like in an instant I came to understand the kinds of books that used to cause me to think, *Ah, what is this stuff? What is this guy talking about? Who does he think he is? Who is he kidding?* Now I read them, and I get it. I see things in a totally different way.

As you begin to awaken, you'll have all kinds of instantaneous new approaches and ways of looking at things, because you're eliminating the rigidity that you previously had. The highest form of ignorance is to reject something you know nothing about. Yet some people go through their whole lives like this, constantly blocking the new from coming in, lest it conflict with their firmly held beliefs. For the rest of us, the openness is available in an instant. And that "instant" can happen anywhere: It can happen at a lecture. It can happen at a church service. It can happen in a beautiful encounter between another human being, maybe even a stranger. It can happen in any number of ways because you are now open. That openness gives you the opportunity to understand things that were always cloudy for you before.

The boundaries between yourself and other people start to break down because you realize that we're all one. I recently got something really beautiful in the mail: It was a picture of the planet, with writing around it that said, WHEN YOU UNDERSTAND THAT THE WORLD IS ROUND, YOU CAN NEVER CHOOSE UP SIDES. That is so true, as is the fact that we all live on this one planet. But you've got to get back far enough to see the oneness that we come from, the oneness that we are, the oneness that all humanity is—that we are like one cell in this whole body called humanity.

You no longer notice the things that once separated you from other people. All of those boundaries have become diffused, and you view each human being you meet not in terms of what separates you from them, but of what connects you to them. You only see that connectedness, which gives you the motivation to build bridges instead of walls. Rather than clinging to your separateness, you now reach toward others. You see everyone out there as connected to you in some way.

What really happens here is that your personal identity changes. Again, labels no longer apply. You are no longer a writer, a husband, a father, or whatever it is—you are now a higher consciousness, and other people are with you. They may be on a different place along the path of life than you are, but you don't have to separate yourself out from them.

Certain activities and events that formerly carried meaning and motivated you are also no longer important. Think back to some things that were so crucial to you at an earlier time in your life, like whether you belonged to the right club, whether your friends liked you, whether you had the right dress or the right suit on, whether you showed up at the right gatherings. What does it feel like to consider these activities and events that once carried a lot of meaning for you, now that they no longer do? What new joy did you find to take its place? Maybe you'd rather be by yourself or with one person whom you love, doing something as simple as reading a poem or going for a walk.

You don't feel that you have to go through certain motions in order to prove your humanity anymore. It's all okay now. You don't have to have a date every Friday and Saturday night. You don't have to be attached to a mate at all. You don't have to earn anything. You don't have to concern yourself with all of these things that take up so much of many people's time and energy.

Don't get me wrong—there's nothing wrong with nice clothes and fun social gatherings. It's terrific and fine if that's what you're doing right now and you're enjoying them. Have a wonderful time with them, please. Just know that as you start awakening—and this can happen at any age, at any time—more things will become less and less significant. You'll find yourself getting to the point where you say, "No, I don't think I'm going to do that. I want to read this." Or, "I'm working on a project. I want to write something that's really important to me." Or, "I've got a painting that I've been working on, and I want to see if I can get that finished." Or, "There's four or five of us starting a new group that's trying to raise awareness about addiction." Or whatever your new passion may be.

Your priorities in life begin to shift radically away from events, activities, things, or places that you used to try so hard to fit into. All of those things that were once so important are gone now. You will now find yourself consulting what I call your "inner signals." That is, you'll follow your own guidance about what is right and what you have to do at all times—you'll no longer look to other people or external factors to show you the way.

I've seen this with my own life, dramatically. The most important times that I have are with my children. When I can't be with them or I choose not to, I find meaning when I'm alone. I increasingly find that the moments I can read, write, draw, or just contemplate my own thoughts are absolutely perfect. The idea of having to go to a movie on Friday night and then out for dinner, or any number of things that were a part of my life for a long time, no longer hold an appeal. Yet I look back on that time as necessary, for it all taught me how to get to here.

As you awaken, your relationships literally change. Some of them will grow deeper, but the number you have starts to shift dramatically. You don't feel like you have to surround yourself with other people all the time, so you reduce the number of acquaintances you have. You relate to a select few people who don't have to agree with you all the time, but are *with* you. You tend to have a smaller circle, for you have less patience for a lot of activities and people around you. You might find yourself with only three or four friends, or maybe even one or two, and this is because you are solidifying the relationship with yourself and seeing yourself as part of something much greater, much more perfect. To that end, privacy becomes something that you're almost consumed with. The need to be by yourself and not have other people around you all the time is vitally important.

Your dependency relationships sour completely, and you become less tolerant of anybody determining anything about what your life is going to be. This is one of the most noticeable and dramatic shifts you'll experience. No one is going to tell you what to do any longer. No one is going to dictate to you how you should be; this goes for at home and on the job. You know yourself to be a person who has a great deal to contribute, and you do that. If other people try to control you, first you react with only love toward them. Then, if that doesn't work, you unobtrusively move on.

Another thing you'll find is that the awakening process is something you can't turn away from. You might think that you can, but then it gets you. You now have an openness to the Divineness, the grandness, and the perfection that you are, and because you're acting in accordance with your higher consciousness, you're only letting the good in.

It's like how an artery that is clogged with cholesterol cannot let in the proper amount of blood. Think of your body being all clogged up inside, with cholesterol or disease or the like—then health or nutrition can't get in. Consequently, you'll gain weight, your energy levels will decrease, your complexion will look worse, and so forth. But once you turn your attention to better choices in nutrition and exercise, being healthy takes over in you, and you don't want to stop it. Once you start feeling better, you know that you can't go back to old habits any longer.

An experience I had on a plane a while ago reminds me of this. The meal I was offered looked like it was made in about 1943. Somebody opened up their package, and it had that chemical smell from processed food. It looked like unidentifiable brown stuff, so I asked the flight attendant, "What is that?"

She said, "Oh, that's chicken."

I said, "I never saw a chicken that looked like that." I looked at all these people around me about to dig in, and I said, "Nah, I'll pass on that. Thank you."

At one time, I used to live on greasy food that wasn't much better. The food didn't change; *I* changed. It's like I let something else in and unclogged myself in the physical domain.

The same concept applies in the thinking domain. You let in new ideas: *There is a positive force in the universe, and I am a part of that force. I can make anything I want happen for myself. I am connected to all of humanity. I live in a perfect universe, where there's a synchronicity and no coincidences. Every-thing that happens does so for a reason, and I am here to learn from it. Forgiveness is a way of life.* All these kinds of higher-consciousness qualities enter into your life, and you can't turn away from them. In fact, you get a little more into them.

Now, you don't become a proselytizer, and you're not trying to convince anybody else that they have to be the way you want them to be. That's actually part of being awakened—you don't have to convince anybody else of anything. You choose to love people for where they are, even if they're doing harm. You focus on getting the earth back in harmony with its perfection instead of worrying about any tumult or disorder. You try to get enough people together who are full of love and peace, so they can go out and positively affect others—until we ultimately have no more war or hatred.

Maybe you used to have thoughts only about yourself and at the expense of everybody else, such as, *It doesn't make any difference. I'm going to get mine before the other guy gets his. It doesn't matter if I cheat or lie, or if I have to be dishonest with anybody. None of those things make any difference as long as I am getting what I'm entitled to.* Such notions will diminish, as your values shift toward this concept of harmony.

You appreciate everything that you have, right here and right now. You don't think in terms of what's missing from your life. You're not defined by *What can I get, and how do I get it?* but by *How can I be internally at peace, and how can I help other people to do that too? How can I serve?* You have only love, and when you start giving that away, you find that, irony of ironies, everything you ever wanted is there in sufficient numbers. That's because you know that you're not going to get it all—you *are* it all.

You are harmony. You are peace. You are love. You are awake.

As you can see, the process of becoming truly awake is very powerful indeed. It will lead to a heightened spiritual awareness, and then to enlightenment. So now that you know what to expect on the course ahead, let's begin our wonderful journey.

CHAPTER 2

TRANSCEND YOUR FORM

I've been looking at my hands a lot lately. I've got great hands, but they're different than they used to be. They've got a few new brown marks that I've never seen before, for instance. I don't know what the hell they are—beauty marks, I guess.

When my kids were little, if I squeezed the skin on the back of their hands, it would kind of snap back like a rubber band. Mine used to do that too, only a little while ago it seems. Now it sort of meanders back. I'll time it: "Four seconds, hmm. Last week it was three."

Now, if I thought that my hands or any part of my body constituted who I am, I'd freak out. Thank God I know that I am not the body I showed up in. Neither are you, even though I'll bet you've been taught that you *are* your body. So you've been watching it, and trying to lift the parts that are sagging and falling. You've been watching the hairs fall out of it. I certainly have. But I discovered that those hairs on the top of your head don't really fall out; they go in. Yes, I just made this amazing discovery: the hairs go in, and then they come out through your nose and your ears. If my kids hadn't gotten me an electric nose-hair clipper, which you can also use in your ears, I would have shoulder-length ear hair today. And why? What do I need it there for?

In all seriousness, one of the motivations for this book is to teach you this very important thing: *You are not your form.* You are something much more magnificent and Divine than your packaging, and having your mind stretched to this new dimension of understanding is cause for celebration.

I believe that we all have the ability to transcend or go beyond our form—that is, to *transform* ourselves. In fact, no human being is ever fully formed; we're always in the process of transformation. Just when we think we're formed, we look in the mirror and notice a wrinkle that wasn't there yesterday, an eyelid drooping a little more, a tooth with a hole in it, or what have you. So there's no such thing as a fully formed person.

You now occupy this particular body, but that's not who you are at all. It's akin to an astronaut's space suit—you have this shell that you occupy for a certain amount of time. The problem is, a lot of people think they are absolutely their packaging. Imagine that you went to the frozen-food section of the grocery store and saw something that had a nice picture of broccoli with almonds on it. You brought it home, took the wrapping off and put it in your little pot of hot water, and started boiling the wrapping. . . . Of course, you'd never do that! You know that the broccoli and the almonds are inside the package; they are not the wrapping itself.

That's the same analogy I have for each one of us: We think we are our wrapping. We get into this package, and we believe that it is more important than what the package contains. What it contains, though, is our ability to be anything that we want and to make almost anything happen that we want to.

IT'S ALL IN YOUR MIND

The human mind has an incredible power to make things happen. I know people who have literally performed miracles on themselves, for instance. I also know people who have been at the depths of despair when some magic happened somehow, and their lives changed.

I have a fundamental belief that *anybody* can turn their life around, though. It never comes down to, *Did I get the right body?* Or *Am I strong?* Or whatever you tell yourself needs to be different to achieve what you want to happen. I really think that whatever form you find yourself in is part of your life's curriculum. This is what you got, so if you judge it, are upset about it, wish it were something else or different, curse it, or find fault with it in any way, then you're keeping yourself from finding God, the Tao, nirvana . . . or whatever word you want to use. Such an attitude keeps you from being truly awake.

Lots of people, however, don't believe they have the power to change things outside of themselves through the way they think. They don't want to accept it; they think they're formed, and that's that. They get up in the morning, they go off and do things the way they think they're supposed to in "work formation," and then they come home and they're in "Daddy formation," and then they're in "friend formation," or whatever it is, all through their whole life. They don't understand that there's something beyond that form.

The awakening process can seem complicated and difficult because we can't see the perfect intelligence that's behind all form. There's an intelligence behind a fish in water. There's an intelligence behind a plant that grows in a certain kind of way. There's an intelligence behind every living thing. We miss that intelligence because we're so preoccupied with,

What can I see? How can I get hold of it? Just because we can't physically grasp what's going on in our minds doesn't mean that it doesn't exist, any more than the wind doesn't exist because we can't get a handful of it.

You can't hold wind, you can't smell wind, you can't touch wind . . . you can only see the results of wind. That's all. You know that wind exists, but nobody's ever seen it. How could you do that? It exists independent of whether you can touch it or not. As you become awakened, free from all the stuff that immobilizes most people—all the anguish, all the depression, all the having to get ahead, all the accumulation anxieties, all the type A behavior that we suffer from—that stuff becomes something in the past that is only thought, and you'll never be knocked around by it again.

What makes you who you are has nothing to do with your body. Sure, you can do lots of stuff with the pile of skin, bone, muscle, and gristle you're in, but you *process* and *experience* it all through your mind. So when you can see that you're much more than this form, you understand that the thoughts you have are things, and they can be changed. You can learn to perceive life in a new way, realizing that how you process everything is the key, and it is always firmly in your control.

THE RULES OF THOUGHT AND FORM

Take a look at all of the things that are important to you, starting with your loved ones. Can you understand that the only way you can ever experience them in the moment is through your mind? You can't do it any other way. You can't get behind their eyeballs and be them. This is the limitation of form. Any outer experience can only be done through thought.

Now, take all of the things that you want to accumulate. You'll see that they just exist in thought as well. You can't *be* a diamond or a new house. You can experience it, but you can't ever actually have it or own it. It is only in your mind that you can do something with it.

The only boundaries that exist are in form. As long as you believe you are form, you're always going to have boundaries and obstacles. Someone once asked me, "What are the obstacles to my achieving full happiness?" I replied, "The belief that you have to have obstacles." That's all.

In other words, anything that you can think, you can achieve. A thought is something that if you get it properly in your mind and start living with it, then eventually what you are imaging for yourself has to come about. We'll talk about this more later in the book, but for now, understand that the connection between thinking and creating something for yourself is not some kind of mystical, hocus-pocus thing. You can learn to optimize this vibrational pattern that we call thought, which is instantaneous. You can literally make anything happen that you want to through your ability to think. You get to this place where you understand *There are no limits on me, because I can think anything I want.*

As you see it, there are new rules. Take cause and effect, which is very important in form: You do this, and it causes that. Physical form is altered by this and that. Well, in thought, you don't have to have cause and effect. If you're doing something in thought, and you want to change the thought to something else, you do. If you're in the United States right now but you want to be in Afghanistan, you just go there. You don't have to fly, get on a ship, or drive—you go there in thought.

In the process of awakening, you begin to see everyone and everything in the universe from this place of no limits. You look at everything that you used to get really hung up on wanting to own, and you say to yourself, *If it's in my life, it's fine; if it's not, that's okay too.*

You wonder how the things that upset you years ago ever could have bothered you. As for the things that you're bothered by now, you will look back on them in a few years and wonder how that could have ever been a part of your life. For example, you might have relationships now that cause you to think, *Oh, how could I ever get out of this? I simply don't know!* Soon you'll look back on them and think, *Whew! Thank God I wasn't formed, and I was able to get back and not be in the place that I was at that time.*

THERE IS ONLY NOW

Even though everything that's ever happened to you up until this moment is in the realm of thought, it is very real for you. While you can't touch or have any of it, you can certainly get quite emotional about it.

It's critical to understand this point: *The whole experience of your past up until this very second is all in thought—and nothing more.* How much sense does it make to regret, be miserable, or feel guilty about something that is pure thought? I mean, think about if I were to say to you, "Let's feel guilty about the outcome of the Peloponnesian War. Let's you and I feel some guilt."

You'd laugh and say, "That happened almost three thousand years ago, what are you doing?"

I'd say, "Well, look at how the Spartans were treated—it wasn't nice. The Athenians shouldn't have done that. It was simply awful. Could we change it by feeling guilty?"

You'd probably say, "Of course not! It's over and done with."

In reality, this morning is just as over as the Peloponnesian War. And as Einstein taught us, there's no time in a linear frame at all. That concept of time is merely something we invented.

As for everything that's going to happen to you from this second on, understand that it is also nothing more than pure thought: You can't touch tomorrow. You can't grab on to your goals. You can't take tomorrow's BMW and drive it. It's all thought. Yet you can also have the experience, within your form, through thought. If your whole past and your whole future are all thought, then all that leaves you with is now. So why would you elect to use up this moment with something like guilt or by ruminating on things that have already happened?

You'll hear psychiatrists talking about "living in the past." But no one can live in the past—we can only live in the now. Similarly, people say, "I worry because I live in the future." But they're *not* living in the future—they're using up this moment being consumed with something that might or might not happen later, over which they have no control. It's such a sensible thing to get rid of that. You might ask how, and the answer is actually quite simple: You just do it. That's all. If feeling guilty doesn't do anything to correct what you're feeling guilty about, stop doing that.

If you believe that you can't control your thoughts—that is, you believe someone else does—then what I want you to do is find out who's putting those thoughts in your mind and send that person to me. I will treat them, and you will get better. Obviously, it doesn't work that way!

You want to be able to say, "It happened. It's over. I've resolved it. I want to be there in the right frame of mind, I don't want to be mad. Let's push it out. I don't want it there." However, a lot of therapists might then reply, "That's unhealthy because you're not really dealing with it." I don't think you have to deal with things all the time in order to prove that you're healthy! Imagine there's a great big pile of cow manure in the street. Now, there are some people who'd say, "Hey, I can deal with that—I'm going to walk right through it." To me, that's pretty crazy. A healthy person would say, "No, I don't have to deal with that. I'll walk around it." And that's what they'd do.

You've got to go around a lot of stuff in your life, including your own thinking, when it doesn't serve you. How do you do this? Well, you just do. *Don't think like that anymore!*

YOU CAN DO IT!

Ask yourself if your life is serving you. If it is, great. But what if you're full of misery and unhappiness, depressed, always chasing things, never satisfied, angry a lot, procrastinating all the time, full of guilt, or any of those kinds of things? If so, I recommend trying to see the illusion behind it.

Just stand back and have one little corner of your consciousness that says, "It really doesn't matter whether I meet the deadline or not. I've already put myself into this act. This is the role that I have chosen since I showed up here. There must be a reason for me to keep choosing it. I'm going to go through the role, but I'm never going to let it destroy me or mess me up in any way. So when I start to get into a lot of type A behavior over my deadlines, or I get myself all upset because the Joneses have something I don't have, or anything like that, then I'm going to stop and ask, 'Why am I doing this?' I can't own anything anyway. I can't take anything with me. All I have is now. All I can do with this moment is live it and enjoy it."

Every single time you find yourself slipping back, believing that the things you're accumulating or trying to get done are really important, stop yourself. Come back to the now. Go through the motions, and don't let yourself get destroyed by them. That's the key.

I remember a particular woman arriving in my office years ago looking for help. She'd been in analysis for years because she chewed her fingernails. Can you imagine? This is a lady who wore gloves everywhere she went to keep from biting her nails.

She told me that she'd been in classic psychoanalysis in which she learned that everything had to do with psycho-sexual developmental stages. Her psychiatrist had convinced her that her nail biting, among her other many neurotic tendencies, had nothing to do with her. He'd said, "You're fixated and have an unresolved Electra complex. You have got to resolve your feelings toward your father and mother. Your issue is a manifestation of some subliminal envy—symbolically, these really aren't your fingers."

I asked her, "Why would you come to me? I believe the total opposite of all that."

She said, "My sister came to you about two years ago, and in four weeks, you got her straightened out."

"I don't know if I can talk to you for four weeks. I'm already bored with your fingernails." She smiled, and I continued. "But I'll see you. I'll see you three times, and then you'll be cured."

She asked me to repeat myself, and I said, "Yes, three times. And you can talk about it and analyze it all you want between now and when I see you again. There's only one thing you can't do."

"What's that?"

"You have to keep your fingers out of your mouth."

She started getting very nervous. As soon she got nervous, of course, it didn't matter if she had an oral fixation or an Electra complex, her hands were going into her mouth. So right away, I said, "Get your fingers out of your mouth," and I went to grab her hand.

She said, "You know what? Nobody ever explained it to me quite like that before."

"The fact is that no matter how you analyze the problem, how much you think and talk about it, if you're going to quit biting your fingernails, you've got to keep your fingers out of your mouth," I told her. "There's no other way. Honestly, you can *try* forever, but if you put your fingers in your mouth, you're still a nail-biter no matter what."

And you know something? The answers to almost everything are that simple. I get accused all the time of being simplistic, when I guess there are a lot of people who would rather make things complicated. I like taking complicated things and making them as simple as possible. After seeing me three times and keeping her fingers out of her mouth, sure enough, this woman was no longer a nail-biter.

Think about if you want to do one of the things that people find most difficult: quitting smoking. Well, you can call yourself an oral person. You can go to a clinic and try all the medicines, all the fads. You can put holes in your cigarettes and gradually give yourself a hernia from straining to suck before you get even one puff. You can do any number of things, but ultimately, the only way you'll ever quit smoking is to stop putting cigarettes in your mouth, one day at a time. There is no other way. When I'm asked what the secret to quitting smoking is, I say, "Just for today, don't put any more cigarettes in your mouth."

Your first reaction might be disbelief: "How am I going to do that? What if the urge comes?"

"There is no urge out there. It's really you telling yourself, 'This is too hard, I don't want to do that.' Stop doing that!"

Likewise, stop telling yourself, "This is the hardest thing

I ever did," or even, "It's the easiest thing I ever did." The only thing you can't do is put a cigarette in your mouth. Follow this one simple rule, and you will be an ex-smoker, just like that. That's how it works. In fact, that's the only way it works.

Remember, you can be anything, you can do anything, you can go anywhere. You can learn to sort of watch your form go through all kinds of things. But the Divine part of you, the *real* you, stands back and says, "These are the motions I'm going through, but that isn't really me. I'm much bigger and grander than all of that." You look at your relationships, and you realize that almost everything you fight about isn't even real for you. What's real is how you think—what you fill yourself with. If your thoughts are only of harmony, ease, serenity, and love, then that's all you'll have to give away to others.

When you tap in to this truly awakened part of yourself, you see the perfection behind everything that you're doing. You never worry again about your form wearing out, or about dying, or about any of those things. You know that thought is an endless energy that goes on and on. Most of all, you know that *that's* who you are—not an aging and ever-changing form, but that which is eternal and changeless.

CHAPTER 3

FOCUS ON
THE BIG PICTURE

I remember being on a flight in which the very caring staff were doing all they could to comfort a distressed fellow passenger. The plane was not in any danger, so I couldn't help but be struck by how terribly frightened he was of crashing. You see, when you become truly awake, death isn't anything that frightens you. You know that everything is always in transition—that's the nature of our universe.

I've found that most people who have had near-death experiences say something along the lines of, "It taught me the most valuable lesson of my life, which is that I've got to take each day I have and make the most of it."

The problem is, it shouldn't have to take a brush with death to do something so natural, so basic, and so simple—which is to live your life the way you want to, without having to answer to anyone else. So instead of that old slogan, "Today is the first day of the rest of your life," take on the idea of, "Today is the last day of your life, so live it as if you don't have any more."

The truth is, we don't know how much time we'll have. The past is over for all of us. The future is promised to none of us. All we get is now, and most of us know someone who

THE POWER OF AWAKENING

was wiped out in a silly accident, who dropped dead of a heart attack, who was taken at a young age. Every single one of us is going to have to face a last day, and we cannot predict when that day will come.

Death is as important a part of life as living is. Yet we're careful not to tell death jokes, make an offhand remark about somebody who recently died, or the like. If only we could get to the point where we see death as just another transition, where we leave this dimension that we live in and enter a new one. If only we could understand that we are, in fact, multidimensional! Understanding that and leading life on those terms can be the most freeing, exhilarating, exciting thing that we can do.

THE VERY ESSENCE OF WHO WE ARE

One of the most amazing insights I ever had was when my grandmother died. When she was admitted to the hospital, one of the things they did was weigh her for some reason. I guess they had to have it in their records, or maybe you don't get into heaven if you don't have a weight certificate. I don't know what hospitals are thinking with all this record keeping. I always wonder about all the people who died before we had records. Whatever happened to all of them?

Anyway, my grandma was 95 years old and weighed 133 pounds when she entered the hospital. We knew that she was very close to dying, and we watched as the life literally left her body. Then her package—the bones and skin and hair, all that stuff that certainly wasn't my grandmother—grew cold and stiff. They weighed her for the death certificate, and she was 133 pounds, exactly the same. So whatever it was that constituted her life, her very essence, was invisible and weightless. It couldn't be weighed or measured. That's true for each and every one of us. What our life is really all about defies the world of form, yet we spend so much of our energy and time here, in this part of our consciousness, that we believe this is who we are.

This makes me think of our sixth president, John Quincy Adams. He was a man who was highly spiritual and very intelligent. I think he had perhaps the highest intellect of anyone who ever sat in the White House. For example, he rejected slavery while many of his contemporaries practiced it. This is what he wrote about himself a few days before he died, in a letter to a friend:

> John Quincy Adams is well, but the house in which he lives at the present time is becoming dilapidated. It's tattering on its foundations. Time and the seasons have nearly destroyed it. Its roof is pretty well worn out. Its walls are much shattered and tremble with every wind. I think John Quincy Adams will have to move out of it soon. But he himself is quite well, thank you.

Once we understand that we are not the "houses" we're currently in—that is, our bodies—then fearing death becomes impossible. After all, we know that we can't kill thoughts, because thoughts are energy. We can't kill feelings, which are the result of thoughts. We've also established that our bodies change form all the time, but who we are as human beings consists of the entire mental process. Who we are comes from the way we think and process our world rather than how our bodies take shape (and, eventually, lose their shape). When we're awakened, we look at death as absolutely necessary and nothing to fear.

You only fear what you don't face, and what you don't face will control you. If you have the courage to face your fear of death, you'll come to understand that everything you experience in life is a mental image. I can never look out and see the world the way you see it. I can never be your liver or kidney, no matter how much I care about you. I can't be the process that you are. You begin to see that you are not that liver or kidney either; you are your unique perceptual approach to everything in life. You are your thoughts, and those never die. In fact, nothing that has life in it, that has that intelligence, that perfection in it, dies. It's simply in transition.

Returning to the topic of my grandmother, I know that there's nothing that could have ever killed her. I know that the essence of my grandmother couldn't have died. Everything she accumulated and needed and had to do in her 95 years, which she could now see from a different level of consciousness, was all an illusion. It was all just *stuff* that she was going through, which she was creating in a different dimension.

As I've said, we are multidimensional human beings. One of the dimensions we experience is form, but there are many other dimensions to us as well. Just try to imagine that. If you can't—if it's too woo-woo, metaphysical, philosophical, or tough for you to get hold of—you might be surprised to find out that you've already experienced this for a third of your life.

YOU LEAVE YOUR FORM ALL THE TIME

People often ask me, "Where do you think we go when we die?"

I respond, "Where do you go when you are asleep?"

In other words, when we go to sleep, what do we do? We leave this dimension called form and go into a nonform dimension. We are in pure thought the whole time, and it's all fine. None of us are troubled about transitioning into sleep, nor do we wake up saying, "Whew! I was so frightened that I was in this dream and going to stay there!"

Let me tell you how the rules are different when you're asleep and in nonform: There's no beginning or end. There's no cause or effect. There's no time. There's no life or death. For example, you may have had the experience of being asleep and feeling the presence of a dead loved one right there with you. Or you may have experienced being younger than you are in your dreams. If you're 18 again, you look and feel like you're 18, don't you? I have this horrible dream that I'm back in the Navy, and they forgot my discharge date. I can't get anybody to acknowledge that I've done my four years, so it's time for me to be out. I've got to go home, go to college, get married, have kids, and get on with my life, but everybody's telling me, "I can't find your records." It's so vivid!

In that third of our life when there's no time or space, when there are no limits of any kind, it's very real. Our bodies are dramatically affected by the thoughts we're having, and we transcend our form at that time. And one of the reasons we dream is to teach us that every obstacle we run into is an opportunity. In our dreams, everything that we need, we create.

Imagine driving along on a beautiful day, when all of a sudden the road ends and there's a cliff. So what do you do? Somehow you sprout some wings. You think, *I'll fly over this,* and that's exactly what you do. You create out of that obstacle whatever you need. If you're underwater and have to stay there for an extended length of time, that is no problem— you just get yourself some gills and stay under there.

Dreaming is one way you can get a handle on another level of consciousness, because you enter a new realm when you go to sleep. When you dream, you live in another world, one of pure thought. You can do anything, and you create everything you need. You don't say, "Oh, I didn't have a body. That was an illusion." Because if somebody's coming at you with a knife, even if it's a dream, your reaction to it is real. When you wake up, your heart is really pumping, but you can also look back and say, "That's an illusion; there was nobody with a knife."

There are many ways in which the experience of what you're dreaming manifests itself in your body. One interesting phenomenon that demonstrates this concept is politely called a nocturnal emission. This is so fascinating to me because you would think that in order to have a sexual experience, you'd need to have some kind of physical contact. But you're asleep when you have this experience; it's happening purely in the world of thought, even though effects can be seen in the world of form. In fact, even when two people are having an actual sexual encounter, it's all still thought. The largest sex organ that we have is our brain.

It's all done through thought. If you can't think it, and you can't get the image, then you can't make it happen. So the dance of life is possible through thought and nothing more. That is, the very stuff of life is thought.

THE LEVELS OF CONSCIOUSNESS

There are different levels of consciousness, which can be envisioned like a stepladder with only three steps: The bottom rung of the ladder is dreaming consciousness. Then the next rung up is your waking consciousness, which is what we go through most of the time. The final rung is another level of consciousness beyond the waking consciousness, which we'll call a question mark for now.

When I was a kid, I had some bizarre experiences on the lowest rung of the ladder because people could talk to me while I was dreaming. My brothers used to get our mother or other family members to come over to watch what would happen. They'd say, "Look at this guy." One time my oldest brother, Jim, gave me a bedsheet and said, "You're going to school, Wayne. Here's your shirt. Come on, get it on." I was trying to get my arm into this sheet, but there was no arm-hole, of course, so I had this crazy thing going. Jim was saying to our mother, "Look at him; he thinks he's getting dressed."

Another time, I was dreaming about shoveling snow. I asked out loud, "Where's my shovel?" Jim said, "Here's your shovel, Wayne. Go ahead and take it." He was on the second rung in waking consciousness, talking to me in dream consciousness. I was in a different level of consciousness, so the dream was real for me. As long as my brother would cooperate with me and pretend to be with me in the dream, then I would stay with it. But if he would've said, "You're crazy, you're dreaming, just wake up," I would've either gone deeper into my unconsciousness or come out of it and realized that there was no shovel. Of course that's what eventually happened: I woke up and again asked, "Where's my shovel?" Jim said, "Oh, you're awake." I realized I didn't have my shovel, but I'd had the *experience* of having it. It all seemed incredibly real.

The only time you know you're dreaming is when you're awake. So you have to wake up to know that what you were just doing was an illusion. That's the difference between the dream-consciousness level and the waking-consciousness level. What I suggest is that in order to go from one level of consciousness to another, you have somebody who's on the second rung go down there and pretend to be with you on the first rung.

Now we get to the third rung, which has the question mark. What is that level of consciousness, and how is it different? I believe that if somebody from that level of con-sciousness wanted us to know what is possible for us at a higher level than we're living right now, they would have to be here among us. Much like my brother speaking to me from waking consciousness to my dream consciousness, that person would pretend to be with us in the dream. Someone from another level of consciousness would show us that we don't have to live this illusion, and then they'd leave to another dimension.

This is what I think highly spiritual people do: They clearly see the illusion. They know that the *experience* of the illusion is real, but it can't be, in fact. We can't own anything, we can't have it, we can't get hold of it.

There are many highly spiritual people on this planet right now who understand this higher level of consciousness. They help us along as they try to get us to see that there's a higher place we can get to. That higher place isn't form; it's transformation. When we get that, then we can go in and out of this next dimension . . . and then the next dimension . . . and the next. . . .

YOU CREATE EVERYTHING YOU NEED

When I was a child, I realized that the shovel that had been handed to me was an illusion, but my experience of it was very real. I believe that when we die and leave our form, we will also be able to look back and see the illusion of all that we've accumulated and held on to, all of our "shovels"—the money and things that we can't take with us—and understand that we created everything that we needed in the level we're at now. We created it all. If we needed a partner to fight with every day, then we created that. If we needed to have poverty for some reason, then we created that.

For me, this is the essence of life. I know that there are higher dimensions than this waking-consciousness level that we live in. I know that I can live the illusion and enjoy it all, make it all work for me. I create whatever I need. If I need to have a house full of children, I create that. If I need to have an experience of losing my keys, I create that too. I've created everything that happens in order to make this level of consciousness work.

Now, suppose you went to sleep and had a dream in which you had all this money and everything you ever wanted. Then you woke up but were still attached to the stuff that you had in your dream: "Wait a minute, I want that. There was gold there, there were all these friends, I had a Ferrari there. I've got to have all of this now!" Somebody would come along and say, "Sorry, that was a dream. You can't be attached to that; it was only a thought you had." Well, that's the way you've got to view life. Instead of being in an eight-hour dream, you're in an 80-year or a 90-year dream. At the end of the dream, you don't want to be looking back at all the stuff you wish you could still have. Because you *can't* have it—none of it will ever actually be yours.

As absurd as it would be for you to be attached to the stuff that you had in your dream, it's equally as absurd for you to be attached to the stuff that you're having in *this* dream. In fact, when you get to a higher level, you'll look back on all this and ask, "What did I need any of that for?"

There is a place in our waking consciousness that is similar to our dreaming consciousness, in which there's nothing to limit us. This is the state of the *waking dreamer.* We are not the bodies that we carry around or our possessions, which are all just things that we have created because we need them for the dream. Yes, in this dream the things that we need we also create. The trouble is, we don't want to call it a dream because it's so real. And yet, that is exactly what it is.

You may have had a similar experience to this: You're having a great dream, when something from another dimension wakes you up—a bell goes off, a door is slammed, the phone rings, whatever it may be—and you sort of half wake up and come back into your form. You leave pure thought and all that great stuff you can create, and you say to yourself, *I want to go right back to sleep so I can find out how this dream turns out.*

When I bring this up with audiences, I'll ask, "What's going on here? If you're creating this dream, then why would you ever need to go back to sleep to find out what the outcome was? You're the one writing it!" It would be like me sitting down to write a story and wondering how it's going to turn out. If you asked me who was writing this story, I'd say, "I am." You'd point out, "Okay, if you're writing it, then you must know how it's going to come out." I'd then say, "Yeah, I've got it all outlined, so I guess I do know how it's going to come out." I mean, if I'm writing it, then I can create whatever I want.

So how do you explain what's happening when you're trying to get back to a dream? Who's writing the script, if it's not you? Well, you have entered a new dimension with different rules, in which you are now playing a new role. You've entered a dimension that's already been written, and you do this all the time—this wonderful dimension of thought is right there for you.

Did it ever occur to you that you are creating everything you need for *this* dream? That when you finally leave your form this time around, you're going to look back and see that the attachment you have to all your stuff is just as much of an illusion as the knife the guy had in your other dream? Sure, it's real while you're experiencing it, but when you look at it from a transformed point of view, it doesn't exist. When you have awakened, you'll get this—you'll realize that this is all a dream.

All of us have roles that we play: I'm a rent-a-Wayne Dyer. You're maybe a rent-a-Marjorie, a rent-a-Sally, or a rent-a-George. But when we are truly awake, we realize that they are only roles, illusions. It doesn't mean that we don't enjoy them. Why wouldn't we enjoy our dream? We're creating it, after all.

If your dream isn't satisfying or fulfilling to you, you can make it be so. All you have to do is change your thought, because that's all you are. So you can watch yourself, like an actor. You might say, "Jeez, that was a funny thing I did this morning, and it was really stupid. I don't think I'm going to do that anymore." You stand back and watch yourself do all these things, knowing that your Divineness, who you really are, is beyond what your form is doing. When you understand that, then the rest of the dream becomes whatever you want it to be. Remember, you can create anything you want now for the dream, and you do so through thought.

THE PATH TO UNDERSTANDING

The ultimate transcending of our form is what we call death. I don't pretend to have a handle on the great mysteries of the universe, but I have no fear of death whatsoever because I know that you can't kill thought. We are thought; thought can never be destroyed. Therefore, we can never be destroyed. Thought is the ultimate vibration in the universe, which goes on forever. It's an endless thing.

Everything is programmed into a single little drop of protoplasm, all that you'll ever need, for your entire life, in the form that you're in. It's all a mystery, and while we are dreaming it is unlimited. There are no limits to what you can do while you are dreaming. You can be anything, you can do anything, you can go anywhere, you can be any age, and it's very real. You experience it very dramatically. You're not ever afraid to go to sleep, so why be afraid to change this form? It's just part of the "isness" of it all.

Everything that's happening is supposed to be happening. Even our desire to eradicate the things that we see as unpleasant is part of the Divine plan—that's part of the paradox you have to understand. F. Scott Fitzgerald wrote a wonderful essay that said something like the highest form of intelligence that you can get to is when you're able to have two contradicting concepts present in you at the same time. He explained that it is perfectly legitimate within the context of this perfect universe to think everything is hopeless and yet have hope at the same time. To know that there are people who are starving and be determined to do something about it at the same time. And the reason I believe that what he says is true, that this contradiction is the highest place you have to get to, is because each one of us is a paradox as well.

We live with two different sets of rules: We live in form, which has its own rules, and we live in nonform, which has a whole other set of rules. We're in this one package, but there's always this dualism. We simply have to keep our focus on the big picture.

The path to understanding the big picture is different for everyone, but its availability is there. By the big picture, I mean knowing in your heart and soul that there's more to life than what your body is going through, and knowing that there's nothing worth getting yourself all bogged down and depressed and worked up about. You have a new intelligence. Noticing that new intelligence can lead you away from any fear of death and into your true potential, for happiness and fulfillment in yourself. You know it all and see all that.

If it takes a brush with death in order for you to get that big picture—to be able to relax in the face of conflict, to not allow yourself to get stressed out over small things, to enjoy your present moments and find fulfillment and joy in them—then have that near-death experience, but have it in your mind only. One of the ways to accomplish this is through meditation; another is through visualization.

Imagine yourself participating in your own funeral in your mind. See yourself dying of a horrible disease and suffering. Go through it. Experience that whole thing, and as you do, this concept will arise naturally for you: *This doesn't have to be brought into form . . . I can act it out in my mind like a dream, live through it, really get the feeling of it, and then decide I don't have to bring this into my form any longer. I can make a decision not to do it.*

Whatever it takes for you is fine. All I'm saying is that you don't have to go through it in the world of form, in your physical world. You can transform, go beyond your form. You can be metaphysical, go beyond the physical. Experience it in your mind where there are no limits. You can literally be anywhere through your thoughts. Then when you come out of it, realize that *Okay, that's enough. I've done that now. Let me practice the big picture. Let me see it isn't anything that I actually have to bring into my life.* Once you're able to do that, once you can create that for yourself, then you get all the benefits of the big picture.

DIE WHILE YOU'RE ALIVE

I'd like to share a wonderful, ancient tale with you.

There was this hunter who would go to Africa every couple of years, and he would bring home animals as prizes. One year he discovered a large enclave inside a jungle that was filled with beautiful multicolored parrots, and they all talked. He couldn't get over it, so he captured one of the parrots and brought him home. He took great care of the parrot and talked to him every day, but he did keep him in a cage. Two years went by, and he told the parrot, "I'm going back to Africa. Is there anything you would like me to say to your friends in the jungle?"

THE POWER OF AWAKENING

The parrot said, "Yes. Tell them that I'm very happy in my cage here with you. Just tell them that."

The hunter went back to the place in the jungle where he had captured the parrot two years before. He told the other birds, "Your friend whom I took back has a message for you, which is that he is happy in his cage with me." Upon hearing that, a bird on one of the branches keeled over instantly.

When the hunter returned home, he told his parrot what had happened. He said, "I went back and did what you asked. The moment I told them what you said, one of your friends was apparently so upset and missed you so much that he dropped dead." At that, the parrot in the cage also keeled over. His legs went straight up in the air, and he went stiff.

The hunter was beside himself and couldn't figure out how this could've happened. Before long, he took the dead parrot out of the cage and put him on the woodpile. The second the parrot landed on the woodpile, he flew into the trees.

The hunter said, "What is this? I thought you were dead. You tricked me!"

The parrot replied, "My friend was sending me a message. He told me by his actions that in order for me to escape from my cage, I had to die while I was alive."

This is an old story that's been repeated countless times over the years, so what does it all mean? Well, don't you see that the whole planet is a cage? We're all restricted by the limitations placed on us as human being. We're stuck in our homes or our jobs, and we're all in cages. Even though we have more room to manipulate our circumstances than that parrot did, we're still trapped.

Now, how do you escape from the cage that you're in? You have to see the big picture and die while you're alive. All of us are going to die, so why not experience it in advance? See yourself out of your body, gone, but able to look back at what's going on now. It's much like the dream where you have everything you want, but you're able to look back at it from a greater perspective. In the process, you'll see the folly, the absurdity, of hanging on to anything, of being attached to anything, of needing anything, of telling yourself that you can't be happy without something, whatever it may be.

As soon as you can look back on this like a dream, as soon as you can experience yourself as formless and multi-dimensional, all the things that you cling to become irrel-evant. They're no longer necessary. You have a whole new way of living, a new way of being. It's quieter, it's easier, it's less demanding, it's less painful. There's less suffering because suffering is all played out in this form; you're some-place else now, you've experienced that. You look back and see the absurdity of all of your attachments, knowing that you can never own anything, and then you sort of flow through life. You're not fighting anything, and it all works nicely, easily, perfectly.

Try to detach yourself from the need to have that stuff now while you're here, while you're alive. You may be sur-prised at the contentment you feel when you realize that you have everything you need, but you don't have to chase after it.

I'd like to make it very clear here that when I say we have to die while we're alive, *it is not a physical act.* This all takes place in the mind. By the way, when people are trained in meditation and in becoming high spiritual masters and so on, they're expected to do this exercise of experiencing their own death, to know what it's like, to feel it inside.

I apply this concept in my own life by reminding myself that an eight-hour dream and an 80-year dream are basically the same if there's no such thing as time. I also remind myself that being attached to anything—in the sense of needing to have it and identifying with it and defining myself by the acquisition or by getting someplace, by those kinds of acts—is absurd from the perspective of my no longer being here in form.

I heard of a philosopher who was asked if there was a God and whether he believed in life after death. He said, "No, I don't believe it; I know it. I absolutely know you cannot kill thought. You cannot kill spirit, you cannot kill the higher consciousness that's part of the eternity. Just like the universal is eternal, so are you."

I feel the same way: When you know that, and live that, then the idea of your form dying becomes less and less scary. So I try to look at everything that I'm doing from the perspective of being able to look back at it, from the point of not being here any longer, from the point of being dead or from looking back at what was in my dream.

While you're in the dream, everything that you're doing is very exciting and very real. It's not like you're going through it and saying, "Oh, this doesn't count, I had my fingers crossed." Even when you are truly awake, you don't look back and say, "I want all that stuff back. I have to have it. If only I would have done things this way." You don't do any of that. You simply move on to the next level. You have a new perspective, and the perspective is that of not needing anything in a very short time. I mean, eternity is just a speck away for all of us, and we won't need any of this stuff.

Again, try to detach yourself now so that you can flow, so that you can be part of that perfection instead of always worrying, hurting, or being angry. All suffering gets played out in form; there's no suffering in thought. A body may be going through all this pain, but who you are isn't suffering at all. So you can get that new perspective of looking back on all this from the vantage point of no longer needing to have or own anything. You know that your humanity, your Divineness, isn't in things and acquisitions—it's in how you think.

THE LAST DAY OF YOUR LIFE

Let's circle back to the phrase "Today is the first day of the rest of your life." I'd really like to change it to "Today is the last day of your life." Now there's a slogan! You don't have any "rest of your life" guaranteed to you at all. What you get is now. You've got to learn that death is like the old joke: it's nature's way of telling you to slow down. Sure, it'll do that. But all kidding aside, you've got to get things in perspective.

Life itself is an unfinished-ness. It's not like you're going to get it all organized into the right place, and then check out. No. God doesn't tell you in the morning, "You'll be checking out about 11:30 P.M. You will be joining me tonight." You can't say, "Wait a minute, God. You don't understand. I bought three bottles of shampoo. As soon as I use up that shampoo, I'll be ready. And by the way, God, I've got a whole bunch of steaks in the freezer. I got them on sale and haven't even touched them yet." You don't want to make God mad on your last day. He could say, "Now it'll be about 11:20 P.M, buddy."

I suggest that you get into the habit of telling yourself every morning, "This is the last day I've got." Because you know something? All of us, at some time or another, have got to face a last day. Nobody's leaving here alive. And when you tell yourself, "This is the last day of my life," you get a whole new perspective on the worlds of form and nonform. You know death is merely another transition rather than anything to be feared.

Let's say you're in a traffic jam on your way to work. If you know that this is the last traffic jam you're ever going to get, you're going to enjoy the hell out of it. If this is your last bridge crossing, you'll be checking that bridge out carefully. You'll introduce yourself to everybody in line there: "Excuse me, my name is Wayne Dyer. I'll be leaving tonight, but I wanted to tell you how much I like that bridge there. Boy, is that nice."

There would be no rush. You'd take it easy, and savor your time. Now, why not cultivate that attitude for everything in your life? Keeping your focus on the big picture will help you do just that.

CHAPTER 4

BE AUTHENTICALLY FREE

Did you know that there are two kinds of freedom? The first is one that I call "counterfeit freedom," and it's exactly what the word *counterfeit* means: phony. It's not authentic. It's not real. Yet so many in our society pursue it relentlessly.

Some of the most popular forms of counterfeit freedom come from drugs or alcohol. People pursue such substances in order to feel high, to feel giddy, to feel euphoric. These days, both legal and illegal drugs are widely available everywhere. It's gotten to the point that in virtually every metropolis and even tiny villages across the world, we can find generations of people hooked on these substances.

The reason this is a counterfeit freedom is because you can never get enough of it. With a drug, you spend most of your time chasing your high. You briefly feel euphoric and free, and then a few moments later you say, "I've got to have some more of that."

Obviously if you really were free, you'd experience a sense of contentment rather than needing anything else.

The test of authenticity is whether you need more of something in order to keep feeling free. If you do, then you are not free at all. This thing owns you, and you are its prisoner. You don't have it; it has you. It is not something you're using; it is something that is using you. Before long, you're using it again, and then again, and again—you can never get enough of what you don't want.

Yes, it is ironic that the things we don't want are the ones we chase after. We really don't want these drugs, we really don't want this alcohol in our system, yet we find ourselves constantly chasing after it and never getting enough.

This search for freedom through substances has trapped users into a lifestyle of never getting enough of what they don't want. They think they'll be free when they experience the fantastic high that comes with the drug or drink, but the pleasure is only physical. It lasts a moment or two, then there's the demand for more.

Authentic freedom, on the other hand, doesn't demand any more. When you experience this freedom, you're not going to say, "Oh, I'm not satisfied. I have to have more." Instead, you'll have a blissful sort of feeling—the freedom of knowing your higher self, of knowing God.

Authentic freedom causes you to feel a sense of, *I am here, this is it, I've got it.* Anything that demands more from you, puts you in debt, places your health in jeopardy, or makes you enslaved to addictive powers is a counterfeit freedom.

In this chapter, you'll learn more about authentic freedom, which I define as one in which you're focused on purpose and serving others, not thinking about yourself and how things affect you. The whole idea of authentic freedom is exquisite to me, as it seems to be something that most of us haven't even considered as a possibility for ourselves. I know that it is absolutely possible for each and every one of us. The way to attain this freedom is through higher awareness, which is something very different from what most of us have experienced so far in our lives. It is another wonderful result of being truly awake.

A NEW AGREEMENT

The higher part of yourself is not tied to the world of form. In fact, it has no boundaries to it at all. I call this being in nowhere. Think of when you're born, and suddenly you go from *nowhere* to *now here*. It's the same concept. Nowhere to now here, which is your life, and then back to nowhere. But your awareness—this higher part of yourself, who you really are—was in nowhere, it's in now here, and it'll be with you when you go back to nowhere. That which was never born never dies.

So we arrive from nowhere, somehow and in some mysterious way. I don't claim to know how that happened— I don't have a clue. I'm part of the same process that you are. I showed up here the same way you did. We all go from nowhere to now here, surrounded by eternity. As we've already learned, the higher part of ourselves is eternal, changeless, and formless. The part of us that is not eternal is our form, our packaging, and it is constantly changing.

Before we show up in now here, we essentially sign an agreement concerning what is going to constitute our reality in this form. The agreement says that there are certain things that we can do and certain things that we can't do— we can only accomplish so much, we can only run so fast, we can only do so many things, and so forth. We are then given a whole host of very well-meaning sponsors, such as our parents, our neighbors, our teachers, our coaches, our spiritual counselors or priests or ministers or rabbis. They all have good intentions, but they reinforce that agreement with *their ideas* of what our limitations are, what's possible or not possible for us.

The story for most of us is that we've been doing the steps that we've been shown by well-meaning parents, schools, religious training, and the like for our entire lives. I'm not here to question any of this; it's all according to the Divine plan. But in order to get to that place where we can manifest miracles, we must understand the steps that we've been shown, so we can erase them without judgment.

I'm offering you the opportunity to write a new agreement now, changing the one that you made so long ago. Furthermore, this new agreement is going to involve your coming up with some ideas, behaviors, strategies, and other things you've probably never even considered before. You have to let go of all the stuff that you've been taught. Instead, ask yourself things like: *Can I be in more than one place at the same time? Can I shape-shift? Can I communicate telepathically with someone who isn't in the room? Can I read auras? Can I defy gravity? Can I enter the dreams of another person?*

For those of you who absolutely know that such things are not possible, go ahead and put down this book now. Because we're going into a new realm here. I mean, I'm not just coming out of the closet with this spiritual stuff—I'm ripping the door off as I get out there. Because I *do* absolutely know that these things are possible, and it's that knowing that I want to get into your heart.

Again, I ask that you be open to the ideas I'm presenting here. Try telling yourself, *Maybe I've got to consider changing this agreement that I signed. After all, it doesn't give me a sense of what I really want for myself. My heart says I want something much more. I want to feel that my life is deep and rich and fulfilling, and I want to be on purpose at all times. I want to be able to experience that glowing inner light, that love that so many of the spiritual masters talk about, and I haven't gotten it by doing what I've been doing so far. I can appreciate my past, as it all had to happen in the way it did to bring me to this point. But I have the power to change where I go from here.*

Who you are, whether you know it or not, is a "fringe dweller." That's a term coined by one of my very favorite people, Stuart Wilde. He certainly lived up to his name—he was as wild and wonderful and noble and beautiful a soul as I have ever known. Stuart wrote about the fringe dwellers in his book *The Whispering Winds of Change,* which is one of the best and most profound things I've ever read in my life.

Stuart describes the fringe dwellers as those who have left the system spiritually and instead reside in a sort of neverland area where they are no longer concerned with having to fit in or having to be like everybody thinks they should be. They're people who have love in their hearts and don't want to buy into the antagonism and the hatred and the bitterness and the strife that so many people seem embroiled in.

It's actually a large group that you find yourself in. There's a real hunger for what you believe in, as there's an incredible spiritual deficit in the world. *That's* the true deficit, not the one of money that we hear about. We fringe dwellers are the ones who are creating the consciousness that is going to transform the world. The changes that we have seen taking place all over the planet in an extraordinary spiritual renaissance are coming from the way that we have decided to process our world. We are no longer going to be a part of a system in which we have to subject ourselves to the evils of nationalism and competition. We are going to choose something new.

SUSPEND YOUR DISBELIEF

If you're having difficulty with what I've been discussing in this book, it might be because you haven't learned how to experience what's called "the willing suspension of disbelief." This is what you do every time you go into a movie theater. When you settle into your seat, you know in your heart that what you're seeing is coming from a projector in the rear of the room onto a two-dimensional screen, and the story isn't actually happening in the theater. You don't sit there and say, "I'm not buying into *this*. Those are just images that are being projected, and somebody's trying to fool me." No, you willingly suspend your disbelief and say, "I'll allow myself to be entertained and informed, and then I'll pick my doubt back up when I leave."

Well, the same thing applies to what I'm talking about here. Some of it might conflict with the agreement you made with what it is that constitutes your limitations. But keep in mind that any limitations you have imposed on yourself are all in the physical domain of form.

I find it interesting that if someone I'm talking to says that they want to make a change—let's say they want to lose weight, quit smoking, leave their drug habit behind, or have a Divine relationship—it's so easy for me to detect whether or not they're going to be able to do so. Because about two minutes after explaining their desire, they usually come up with a reason why it can't happen: "Oh, that's not possible. No, I can't do it." Then they tend to come up with a list of things they've been told about their limitations by all the well-meaning people in their life.

Similarly, as you've been reading, you may have felt some doubt. You might have said something like, "No, this is not possible. All of this is easy for Wayne Dyer to say, but it's not anything I could accomplish. It can't happen for me." I ask that you willingly suspend your disbelief, at least until you're done with this book. If you want to buy into your disbelief again, much like when you leave the theater and go back to a different reality, then fine. But the more you can allow yourself to open your heart, the more you'll allow good things to enter your life.

Keep in mind that what you think about is what expands, so if what you think about is *It can't happen,* then *It can't happen* has to expand. If what you think about in your relationship is what is wrong, what is missing, or what you don't like, then that will be the nature of your relationship. So once you understand that what you think about is what expands—or as you think, so shall you be—you'll get really careful about what you think.

Everything in the universe is energy, including you. All of the things that constitute your body are really a form of energy. They are just resonating at a certain frequency and appear to be solid because of that frequency. The energy I'm talking about is not that which resonates at the solid form, but another kind that is also with you at all times. This is like having an energy body that is physical and also spiritual. The primary energy that you've been using all your life is what we call this outer, or physical, energy. This is the body's life-sustaining force that allows the heart to beat, the lungs to fill up, the blood to circulate, the process of elimination, and all that.

There is also an inner energy. One of the great teachers of my life was a man named Swami Muktananda. In his book *Mystery of the Mind,* he writes the following about Divine energy, which is the energy I'm asking you to consider:

> One day this light will explode, and you will see it everywhere. You will see the entire universe existing within it. The Divine light of Consciousness will begin to fill your eyes, and then wherever you look you will see it. You will see its radiance in people, in trees, in rocks, and in buildings. You will see the same

consciousness rising and falling in every wave of thought and feeling that passes through your mind; wherever your mind goes, you will find your own inner Consciousness, the creator of the world. You will see that the entire universe is contained within your own Self. You will know that everything—all the infinite modifications of the world—is nothing but your own play. You will realize that it is you who are being reflected everywhere and that it is your own reflection that passes before you all the time.

I'd like to add here that you always have this power within yourself. Remember, you are an extension of Source, which is limitless. All you have to do is make the choice to know this spiritual part of yourself, and you can tap in to it by facing in a different direction than you're used to. Instead of facing out, concerning yourself with what's going on around you, you can face inward and directly contact your spiritual nature. You can then live each of your days, regardless of what you may be doing, with the sense of joy that comes from being on your sacred quest.

It doesn't matter what your form is like. It doesn't matter what you do—whether you decided to be a stay-at-home parent, a construction worker, an accountant, a dentist, or a pizza-delivery driver. None of that really matters. I'm not talking about what you do here; I'm talking about the inner Divine energy that you possess.

WHO'S REALLY IN CHARGE?

Perhaps you can understand all of this best through a metaphor.

I used to love Westerns when I was a kid. I'd go to the Roy Rogers Riders Club and pay my 12 cents on a Saturday afternoon and be thoroughly entertained. In every single one of them, there would be this scene, which I'm sure you're familiar with if you've ever watched an old Western. In this scene, the stagecoach's driver has been wounded and lost the reins, so the horses pulling the carriage are running wild. The driver is no longer in control of the coach, so it's being dragged helter-skelter through the sagebrush.

So here's the metaphor. It's based on something written by Eknath Easwaran in his beautiful book *Dialogue with Death*, which is an interpretation of one of the great Indian stories known as the Katha Upanishad.

The stagecoach is your body. The driver is your intellect. The horses that are out of control are your five senses (sight, sound, smell, taste, and touch). The horses are pulling the stagecoach along, and that's a good representation of what happens to most of us in our lives. Our five senses, which give us such physical pleasure, are pulling our body wherever they want it to go because the driver, the intellect, has been wounded and is no longer in control. The reins between the horse and the coach are the emotions that we have.

Inside of the coach, a lovely lady from Philadelphia, with her nice hat and gloves on, is pleading with the intellect and the horses: "I have a message to tell you. Don't allow yourself to be pulled in this direction. Please stop and listen to me." The lady is your higher self, the spiritual part of you.

Whenever the senses are in charge, there is no intellect, and the emotions are running wild. The taste buds on the tongue weigh less than an ounce, for instance, and yet I have seen that ounce pull a 280-pound man into a bakery. He is looking at these cream puffs, and the lady from Philadelphia is imploring him not to eat this stuff. She's saying, "This is going to kill you! But it doesn't have to. You just lost control for a second, and you can get it back. Leave the bakery, eat some vegetables, and take good care of yourself instead."

Perhaps for you, the lady from Philadelphia pleads, "Don't go into that bar. Don't drink that alcohol. Don't use those substances that are going to destroy you." But here come the horses, and they pull you into the bar. These senses, these horses that are out of control, are running your life. You are not free. Your body is being pulled where you don't really want to go, and the lady from Philadelphia doesn't get paid any attention.

You might say, "I have an alcohol problem." In reality, you don't have an alcohol problem; your horses have an alcohol problem. *You* have a horse problem—you don't have them under control. You are allowing these senses and this external energy to pull you through life and dictate what it is that you should be doing in almost every aspect of your life. You allow it for this temporary amount of pleasure, which is nothing more than counterfeit freedom that you get for a split second. Then it's gone and you're chasing after it some more. The horses are pulling your body and mind through life, and you never listen to that sweet voice inside the coach that is telling you to get your life under control.

There's something much grander and greater available here. So let's regain control of the reins and train these horses to go in the direction that we want them to go, rather than allowing them to pull us uncontrollably. In this way, we can find our authentic freedom.

LISTEN TO YOUR HIGHER SELF

Once you are truly awake, you'll find it rather easy to heed the advice of the lovely lady from Philadelphia. Here are some characteristics that you will notice when your higher self is pulling you through life, rather than the horses.

— **The coincidences in your life are much more meaningful, and you're able to manage them with ease.** This is one of the first things you'll notice as you reach this heightened spiritual awareness. Now, that might sound like a paradox: If it's a coincidence, then it's not something that you manage. If it's manageable, it's not a coincidence. You've long been told that when coincidences happen, you're thinking about something and then it shows up in your life—that is, these are things that you have no control over. I'm asking you to willingly suspend that disbelief.

As you face inward and know the spiritual part of yourself, you'll see these things showing up in ways that you never thought were possible. When you get your life on purpose, are fulfilled, and stay in that celestial light, it's like the universe begins to handle all of the details for you.

— **You become aware of the universal source of energy.** You know that it isn't some phenomenon you've read about; it is a part of what you are. There's a part of you that is watching all this happen, and that Divine energy is who you truly are. It allows you to do all the things that you do in your life because it is your very essence. It is this Divine energy that you start paying much more attention to, rather than the absurd idea that you're somehow separate and distinct from it.

— **You regularly access Divine guidance.** This is like spiritual nourishment, and all the immobilizing fears that you once felt in your life now dissipate and disappear. As you access this Divine guidance, again, you realize that it isn't something that is outside of you but rather is something inside of you as well.

When I was reading through the New Testament while preparing to write my book *Your Sacred Self,* I came upon this wonderful passage that relates to this idea. St. Paul was writing to the Philippians, quoting Jesus: "Let this mind be in you, which was also in Christ Jesus. Who, being in the form of God, thought it not robbery to be equal with God" (Philippians 2:5–6). It can be very powerful to think about the idea that we could have the same mind as was in Jesus, who considered himself in the form of God and thought it not robbery to be equal with God. Of course, this doesn't mean that you *are* God; it simply means that you are an extension of this beautiful Divine energy. If you can allow this to become your guiding light, you'll find it to be one of the real beauties of heightened spiritual awareness.

— **You have a newfound sense of appreciation and awe.** You now focus your inner energy on the beauty that surrounds you and receive the energy from those surroundings. As you become in awe and have an appreciation for it, you'll have an appreciation for that energy being within you. You realize that not only can you access that energy, but it is also something that is within you at all times. You don't have to think of it as something external to yourself.

— **You feel a sense of being connected to everyone, shattering the illusion of your separateness.** There's a wonderful book called *Healing Words* by a good friend of mine, Larry Dossey. He is a medical doctor who has spent his life in hospitals, and the book is about how powerful prayer is in helping to heal patients. He describes the double-blind studies that have been conducted where some people were prayed for and others were not. It was found that the power of prayer—the energy that we feel and direct when we place our attention on the healing of others—is something that really makes a difference in healing. There's a connection that is not visible or something you can get hold of.

With your higher awareness and consciousness, you can tune in to this energy, and then you find yourself able to manipulate it. You can affect how others treat you, you can affect your business, you can affect what kinds of people show up for you to love and what relationships you're going to have. You can even affect how strangers interact with you as you're out there in the world. In fact, as you begin to extend out this inner loving energy, you affect everything and everyone around you.

— **You make a new agreement with reality.** That is, the limits of your perception expand to include another whole world of energy that coexists with you at all times. You'll stop giving weight to the beliefs you've been handed by well-meaning people, which tell you what reality has to be for you. You'll abandon that and open up a whole new possibility of what your reality can be, including things you might never have considered before. The ability to do what you thought was only for sorcerers or tricksters is now your daily reality.

— **You become a waking dreamer.** I really love this idea, which I've touched upon in previous chapters. It means that everything you experience in your dreaming consciousness is something you're able to experience in waking consciousness. That is, you stop with the idea that in order to dream, you have to go to sleep.

I'm not saying that you can go out and pick the right lottery numbers with your higher awareness, but I am saying that you can imagine yourself winning the lottery right now. If you had that experience of having a winning lottery ticket that ensured you got a million dollars a year for the next 20 years, what would it feel like? You might respond, "I would feel free and secure. I would abandon all my fears and eliminate all the doubts I have about my ability to get what I want for myself and my life. I'd be happy—ecstatic."

Well, it is a myth that you have to win the lottery in order to have those things you're describing. You can feel like that anytime, including this very moment. Being authentically free—being unencumbered, secure, and joyful—can easily be had with heightened spiritual awareness. Whatever it is you think you need to be happy, you can have the feeling that goes along with it at will. That's the real beauty.

— **You stop looking to counterfeit freedom.** You don't try to find the solution in anything external, such as alcohol or drugs. You know that whatever it is that you are looking for, you can discover it within. And it is heaven.

I had a T-shirt made up one time that said, You've tried everything else. Now try God. What I meant was this: you may have tried addiction, divorce, bankruptcy, moving, and any number of jobs—it's time to try something else.

When you try the higher part of yourself, you find that whatever the problem is, the solution is to let go and let God. No matter how tough the problem may be, or if it's something silly like how to fix a water faucet or find your keys, the answer is to just let go. You'll find the keys. The way to get the drippy faucet fixed will be there. You *will* find the solution to whatever it is that seems to be the problem.

— **The experience of bliss is very common for you.** The thing that you used to want so desperately—that content, peaceful, loving, joyful, knowing feeling that everything is all right and your life is inspired—is there much more frequently than it was before.

One of the great quotations from *A Course in Miracles* is: "If you knew Who walks beside you on the path that you have chosen, fear would be impossible." That's really what the experience of bliss is. There's a loving, peaceful, delightful equanimity with life that comes from telling yourself, "I'm going to allow my higher self to rule."

— **You become less judgmental and more forgiving.** This is a very important part of this business of heightened spiritual awareness. You understand the simple truth that you do not define anybody with your judgments; you only define yourself. If you judge someone else to be a jerk or a fool or bad, it doesn't make them so. They are what they are, independent of your judgments about them. But your judgments do say something about your need to judge.

As you become more forgiving, you understand that in order to really live the higher spiritual life and gain the authentic freedom that you're looking for, you have to let go of all of the anguish, hatred, and bitterness that you carry around. This is the venom from the bites you've received in earlier parts of your life, and the venom is what's killing you, not the bites. You can't be unbitten, but you can certainly remove the venom.

Imagine you are holding a cup, which represents the anguish and the hatred and the bitterness that you feel. Let's say you hold these emotions toward somebody who abused or abandoned you when you were a child. You are told to forgive and let it go, and asked to pick up the cup again. Someone then asks you, "What do you do now if you want to let go of all that stuff that happened to you in the past?" You say, "I'll simply let go of it." Again, that is what you are told to do.

Now, observe what is happening here. In order to let go of the cup, you first have to pick it up. When you pick it up, you embrace it and you own it. The process of picking up the cup, owning it and embracing it, allows you to then let it go. If you walked away without picking it up, you wouldn't be letting it go; you'd never have owned it in the first place. It wouldn't be anything you had to forgive. If you pick it up, you get to the place where you have what we call the *functional adult response* to it. You don't have the *wounded child response,* which is, "Isn't that awful? They never should've done that and I'm still mad." A functional adult picks it up, deals with it, and then lets it go rather than going through life being wounded.

As you become less judgmental, you genuinely embrace those things and then let them go rather than just trying to walk away from them. That's what forgiveness is really all about.

Those are the most significant qualities or characteristics that you'll have when you embrace your heightened spiritual awareness, but there are many more. The main thing you'll notice, of course, is the joy of authentic freedom. There is nothing to compare with the feeling of being in tune with your higher self.

CHAPTER 5

DISCOVER THE THREE KEYS TO HIGHER AWARENESS

Now I would like to explain in detail the keys to higher awareness, which flow from challenging—or even abandoning—the ideas that we've been handed by society. Once we have removed some of our early programming and conditioning, we can reach this heightened state of spiritual awareness and feel authentically free.

The three keys I describe in this chapter all fit together, with one leading to the next. In each section, I'll also offer some suggestions for implementing these keys in your own life.

KEY 1: BANISH THE DOUBT

We'll begin with what I call "banish the doubt," and it comes first because it is the most difficult to do.

Over and over again, the people I have worked with who have achieved higher awareness have told me that it is not the memorization of a whole series of techniques and strategies that will lead someone to it. Rather, what is necessary is a belief that it is possible. The saying goes, "As you think, so shall you be." It's not, "As you be, so shall you think," which is what so many people do. They allow the circumstances of their lives to determine what their inner world is like, so they find themselves angry, hurt, depressed, sad, or fearful because of external events.

As we've learned, if what we think about is what creates our world, and what we think about is laced with doubt, then doubt is what we'll act on. We won't be able to act on anything else. Unfortunately, most of the things that have been handed to us from the well-meaning people in our lives come with doubt attached to them. This is crucial to understand: if what we think about is that we can't do something, or there's even the slightest amount of doubt that it's possible for us to do it, then that is what we will act upon. As Ralph Waldo Emerson noted long ago, "We know that the ancestor of every action is a thought," so if that thought is one of doubt, then that's what we will act upon. That doubt will keep us from being able to create heightened spiritual awareness, or whatever it is that we want to create for ourselves. Banishment of doubt is critical.

If you have a picture in your mind that you can't do something, and if what you think about is what expands, then you will act on that feeling of *I can't do it.* If you're focused on what you don't like or what's wrong in a relationship you have with someone, and then you wonder why your relationship is a negative one, you must change what you're focusing on. Instead, think about what you love and what is terrific, and watch that expand.

All it takes to banish the doubt is to see the unfolding of God in everyone and everything that you encounter. That's all it takes. If you struggle with this notion, tell yourself, *I don't have to understand. All I have to do is imagine that the judgments I have about people are really doubts.*

When you banish doubt, you can easily detect the energy that is trying to get you to go in a different direction, and you know that no one who attempts to push you off course will have any influence over you. Instead of thinking *Why is this person doing that?* or *Why is this drug showing up again in my life?* or *Why is this temptation here?* you understand that you are encountering one of life's exams. You decide to react with love, and the moment you do, you have a new awareness.

It can sometimes be challenging to remind yourself that you always know what to do, understanding that, *Yes, I am going to act upon this knowing rather than upon the doubt that I've had handed to me.* Everything that is physical is finite, whereas everything that is beyond the physical is infinite. Thus, knowings are infinite, and they are transferred to you—even though you are in a different form now, you still have the knowing, which is eternal. The very basis of what it is that constitutes the ability to banish the doubt is this: learning how to shift your beliefs into knowings. Now you can shift from *knowing about* your higher self to *knowing* your higher self. You have a direct relationship with and can access this loving presence that is always with you.

God is as invisible as air. You cannot touch or see Him, yet you know that He is there because you glimpse His wondrous works and goodness everywhere. You *know* that He is there. That knowing and faith go hand in hand. Faith is a knowing, and it isn't about what other people have handed you and told you to worship or practice. So when you shift to faith rather than using the context of *I have to have physical proof,* you're literally shifting away from a belief and into a knowing.

You must understand that faith is a decision you make internally. The sacred energy that flows through everything in the form of Divine intelligence in the universe will come to be sensed by you as your decision becomes a knowing. Faith then becomes an energy that resides within you at all times.

Here are a few suggestions for banishing the doubt:

— Try an affirmation, which is a positive statement that you repeat to yourself to *affirm* and create what you want in your life. I suggest something like: *I rid myself of my doubts by remembering that there is a valid reason for everything that happens.* A simple affirmation may be all you need to start ridding yourself of doubt.

— Make a decision that you're going to meet the invisible God within, so that you will come to know this loving presence rather than know *about* it. When you shut down your inner dialogue and go to that quiet, empty place within you, it will be much easier for you to do this. (There will be more about how to do this later in the book.)

You've got to learn to create the time and space for being quiet and listening, while doing nothing else—and you must do so on a daily basis if you want to banish this doubt. Allow your moment of reflection to be free from any inner criticism. Remove all doubt that has been handed to you by so many well-meaning people. Open yourself up and pause your skepticism, saying to yourself, "I'm going to willingly suspend my disbelief here for a few moments."

— Practice dreaming while awake. Remind yourself that you do not have to go to sleep in order to dream, and give yourself some time to do so. Dreaming while awake can make you feel limitless. You did it when you were a child— you might have been labeled a daydreamer, but that's what you did. You allowed yourself the free-floating excitement of being able to fly, soar, swim, create, write poetry, or whatever it is that you wanted. You allowed yourself freedom from limitations, from doubt.

There's a wonderful couplet from one of William Blake's poems that goes: "If the Sun & Moon should doubt / They'd immediately go out." What you do when you dream is enter into a state where you leave all your doubts behind. You have to know that it isn't a separate being that goes to sleep at night and is dreaming; it is you. The same being that comes into waking consciousness doubting that you can do something goes into dreaming consciousness knowing that you can. So give yourself regular opportunities for this practice, and you'll become a powerful waking dreamer before you know it.

Keep in mind that doubt is not a product of your higher self, and you can learn to observe it rather than choose to own it. You can become the witness to it, which brings us to the next key.

KEY 2: CULTIVATE THE WITNESS

The second key to higher awareness flows directly from the first. Once you learn to banish the doubt, then you can cultivate the witness. You can't do it before.

I love these words from Kahlil Gibran: "For in truth, it is life that gives unto life—while you, who deem yourself a giver, are but a witness." The witness is a compassionate observer, the part of you that is not in the world of form but rather is watching your form. Learning to cultivate it means that you get outside of yourself and watch what is happening in your life, all from the perspective of being the observer.

If you want to be able to create a life of fulfillment, purpose, and freedom through your heightened spiritual awareness, you must detach yourself from the outcome, as tough as that may seem to be. See yourself as the one who is watching all this transpire, which means that you become the noticer: You notice your mind and all the thoughts that are in it. You notice the things that are going on in your life today, as well as past events. You notice what's happening in the world. All of this, you see from the perspective of being the dispassionate witness.

Then as you take note of your worlds, both inner and outer, ask yourself, *Who is this noticer behind that which is being noticed?* If you do this several times a day, you'll see that you are much more than a body and mind going through the programmed motions of your life. Your realization of your true self as the witness behind that which is being witnessed will bring you to a new dimension of peace and creativity. You'll discover, as you really begin to notice the noticer, that you are so much more than your problems. You are not that which disturbs you. Only your form is suffering; *you* cannot suffer.

The witness is that part of us where we are placing our attention. Where we place our attention mandates what we will see manifesting from the world of the formless. That is, when we cultivate the witness, we'll understand the mechanics of creation. Quantum physics tells us that there are particles so small that no one has ever seen them—the only reason we know that they exist is that they leave traces in what are called particle accelerators. When we observe them, they're there; when we take our attention off them, they disappear. The very mechanics of creation state that whatever we keep our attention and focus on will manifest.

That which we observe moves from the wave state, which is invisible, into the particle state, which is the state of the physical world. It's all energy. We used to think that there was the physical world, which was made up of atoms and electrons and neutrons and protons, and then there was the separate spiritual world. It took a leap of faith to go from the physical to the spiritual, because they were seen as two very different worlds.

We used to think that we had to pray to God, and that was based upon this whole idea of an external deity only available to certain people at certain times. Now we discover the truth of what metaphysicians have been saying for centuries: God is within each of us. Quantum physics has shown us that what we think of as "reality" is nothing more than energy, and that energy is everywhere and in everything, all the time.

No matter where you go, if you want to learn about spiritual awareness, you're going to find the great thinkers asking you the same thing: "Can you learn to witness your life rather than identify with it?" Believe it or not, that's where bliss resides, where higher awareness resides, where authentic freedom resides. You will get that freedom when you've learned to banish the doubt and cultivate the witness.

Witnessing is a beautiful experience. You've learned by now how to witness your body. You know that you're not your packaging, yet you still play games with it: you perfume it, decorate it, insure it, seek shelter for it, and try to get things fixed on it. But you also know that there's someone behind there doing all this. You know that there is some invisible presence within you. You say things like, "I was just saying to myself." Now there's two people there: the *I* and the *self* who is the recipient of whatever it is that you were saying. When you say, "I hurt my arm," are you the arm? Or are you that which is experiencing the hurt?

If I say, "I'm going to wiggle my finger," and then I do it, you wouldn't think that's a big deal. But what if I asked you where the command center is that allowed me to wiggle my finger? You'd say, "Well, if we were to look at your brain, we could see the synapses and neurons that allow you to wiggle your finger." But you would never find anything like a command center, with someone who's responsible for me wiggling my finger.

So you can observe your body, but you don't sit around and worry about it. You're not busy beating your heart right now, are you? You're not filling and deflating your lungs. This is the same attitude you can learn to have with your mind, as you watch your thoughts come and go. When you grasp this, you'll realize that we think we are our thoughts. We think the dichotomy is between the body and the mind, but it's not; the mind and body are the same. The dichotomy is between the body/mind and the *soul:* the spirit, your higher awareness, the witness.

Observation has been used effectively in the area of pain management, especially for people who live with chronic pain. Instead of identifying with the pain, people are instructed to become the witness to the pain. They are asked to notice everything about it: its color, shape, and size; when it appears or doesn't; how it can be relieved. As folks become the observer to their pain, they see that where they place their attention is what they manifest. They find that they can literally manifest an absence of pain by becoming the witness rather than identifying with the pain.

This brings to mind something that happened years ago, when I had a practice on Long Island. One day, I asked a patient of mine, "Are you depressed today?"

She said, "You know I'm always depressed."

"Well, is there any part of you that isn't depressed?"

"No, Dr. Dyer, there's no part of me that is not depressed."

"You mean every organ?"

"Every organ is depressed," she said.

"Are you depressed when you wake up?"

"I wake up depressed, I go to sleep depressed, I'm even depressed in my sleep. Like I said, I'm depressed all the time."

Then I asked her the key question: "Have you been noticing your depression more lately?"

She replied, "Yes, I have noticed it more, now that you mention it."

"Tell me, is the noticer depressed? The noticer *can't* be depressed; it's back there watching it all," I said. "Go there. That's God. When you become the witness, you know God. You literally can watch your thoughts and your whole life. That's all you have to do. Everything will get handled because you know you're not alone. You've got to learn that you are not this thing. You have been watching it."

It took a while, but she was able to use this tool to ease her depression. As time went on, she felt much better. Like my patient, when you learn to identify with the observer, what you're really doing is putting your attention on that which you want to manifest.

Here are some suggestions for learning how to cultivate the witness:

— Repeat this affirmation to yourself on a daily basis: *In my world, nothing ever goes wrong.* To me, this is one of the greatest affirmations I've ever heard. I personally repeat it every day.

— When you find yourself troubled by anything, say out loud, "I am more than what bothers me. I am more than my troubles." This simple statement affirming yourself as something more than a receptacle for troubles will keep you from allowing those troubles to run rampant in your life. You'll come to see that you're not those troubles; you're that which is aware of them.

— Try this exercise:

Go to a quiet place and close your eyes. Think of something that has been bothering you for a time. See it surfacing on the black screen of your consciousness. Notice all aspects of the problem—what it looks like, when it shows up, what you feel when it is on your mind, the pain and fear that you have when it is present, how you have dealt with it unsuccessfully in the past. Think of everything you can that is related to this problem.

Now detach yourself from the problem. Just allow it to sit there on the screen of your mind. Look at it from the viewpoint of the compassionate witness, who nonjudgmentally notices the screen. Watch it like a movie, allowing it to change in whatever way it does, observing it while giving it loving permission to do whatever it wants to do. You will see it change and fade in and out of awareness.

With each change or movement on the screen, remain in the caring-witness mode of knowing the energy will do what it will. This act of observation will often result in a feeling of the problem having dissipated. If that happens, observe that from the position of the caring observer as well.

I practiced this act of observation when I had an injury in my foot, near the big toe, which made it very difficult to play tennis. I kept saying, "This injury is keeping me from doing what I want to do, and I'm really upset about it." When I took the witness stance, I no longer saw myself as having an injury. I attributed the pain only to my body and not me. I shifted to speaking as the witness, saying, "This is not me. It is not my pain; it is my body's pain. I am not my body. My body owns that, I don't."

I placed my attention on that which I wanted to manifest, the mechanics of creation, which was having a healthy foot. The next time I went to play tennis, the injury that had been nagging me for several days, which had been causing me to limp and do all kinds of silly things, was gone.

I can also remember using this witness technique when I was a young man. When I was in high school and college, I worked at a Kroger grocery store in Detroit. These huge trucks would come in, loaded with what seemed like a thousand heavy boxes. I'd often be the only one there to unload the truck, put the boxes on a conveyor belt, and so on. The job was hot and backbreaking.

Then at some point, I taught myself to become the witness. I sort of watched the whole truck and visualized it emptying onto the conveyor belt. Rather than identifying with my body, which had to go through all these motions, I got myself into the position of watching myself do it. The process of observing myself and not identifying with the labor allowed it all to flow smoothly and quickly, and it didn't seem to hurt as much. I created a different kind of energy, a heightened-awareness kind of energy, which gave me strength and the ability to pass time just by witnessing rather than identifying with it.

When you can witness and not identify with all aspects of your life, your higher awareness will allow things that once seemed very difficult to become almost meaningless to you.

— If you find yourself burdened with deadlines and a lot of that type A behavior that so many of us take on in the business world, you can detach yourself from it. You can become the witness to that as well, watching yourself go through whatever motions you have to go through, and slow yourself down. From this noticer perspective, you'll see how absurd all the stress that you've always felt around deadline time is. That's just stuff that's going on in your body; you no longer need to have that stress. The placing of your attention on the dissipation of the anxiety by witnessing it, and nothing more, allows it to go away.

— When it comes to confrontations with other people, I'd also like for you to practice being the witness. Rise above the temptation to make someone else wrong, and instead watch yourself and your opponent from the observer perspective. You'll soon see the folly of engaging in this sort of anxiety-producing behavior, and you'll shift to a more spiritual response.

There's one sentence I've learned to keep in mind that I think has brought me more peace than anything else I can offer you: *When you have the choice to be right or to be kind, always pick kind.* In virtually every confrontation that you ever find yourself in, whether it's with your spouse or co-workers or even with strangers, you always have the choice to be right or to be kind. When you make the choice to be right, what you're really doing is deciding to make someone else wrong, and you're immediately creating disharmony. When you make the choice to be kind, that's your higher self, the witness, speaking.

So rather than saying, "You know, that's the fourth time this week that you've said that. You're always trying to make me wrong—who do you think you are?" you can choose to say, "You know, you make a good point. I've never considered it that way." The witness will have taken over, and you'll eliminate all the worry and stress that go with that altercation. So when you have the choice to be right or to be kind, try picking kind. You'll be able to watch those conflicts easily and peacefully resolve.

— Keep yourself in tune with your inner world. Notice your thoughts, and then become aware of the thinker of the thoughts, the invisible you who is behind the actual thought. A lot of times we believe we are the thought instead of the thinker of the thought. And the thinker of the thought is like the noticer; it's that which is observing.

The mechanics of creation that we are learning through quantum physics says that where we place our attention causes us to be able to manifest from the wave state into the particle state. In other words, if we keep our attention on what it is we want to manifest, we will shift it from a wave state—that is, from a thought state—into a particle state, or form. It's a very intriguing kind of notion, this whole quantum-physics thing, especially when you realize how easily you can apply it in your own life. Just remember that you are that which is observing rather than that which is being observed.

— Take time to appreciate the beauty in your life. Take time to be contemplative. Take time to see that this is a magnificent universe. There is an intelligence to this whole thing, and everything you come across has something that you can appreciate in it. Rather than filling your inner world with criticism, skepticism, doubt, anguish, or pain, understand that you always have a choice. All your thoughts are things that you control. Once you take to heart the idea that what you think about is what expands, you can put your attention and energy on that which you appreciate rather than that which you think is not working well for you. Then you will see these heightened-awareness things manifesting for yourself. It all starts with going within.

KEY 3: SHUT DOWN THE INNER DIALOGUE

The third key to higher awareness is "shut down the inner dialogue." Again, this flows from a pattern: First you learn to banish the doubt. Then, as the doubt begins to dissipate, you have the opportunity to cultivate the witness, which can only be there with an absence of doubt. As you get good at cultivating the witness, you find that the best way to be the witness is in silence. Silence is what you have to learn as you shut down the inner dialogue.

The inner dialogue is nothing more than your inventory of beliefs, which have been handed to you from well-meaning people all your life, and are loaded with doubt. It is a constant reiteration of all these things that have been handed to you that keep you from reaching a sense of purpose or from knowing your higher self. It is your ego at work. We'll discuss the ego at length in the next chapter, but for now, understand that in order to get to a higher place, you need to come to know God, or this loving presence that is with you at all times. You cannot do it when you are constantly at the beck and call of your inner dialogue.

Again, you just observe the thoughts; you don't judge them. This becomes easier to do when you learn to become the witness, because nothing can get to you. I'm telling you, I know. Once you get to that silent, empty, invisible place, you'll know what they mean when they say it's the space between the bars that holds the tiger. It's the silence between the notes that makes the music. You need silence, so give yourself as much of it as you can.

In the Tao Te Ching, Lao-tzu says:

> *Become totally empty.*
> *Let your heart be at peace.*
> *Amidst the rush of worldly comings and goings,*
> *observe how endings become beginnings.*
> *Things flourish, each by each,*
> *only to return to the Source . . .*
> *to what is and what is to be.*
> *To return to the root is to find peace.*
> *To find peace is to fulfill one's destiny.*

There are an awful lot of profound thoughts about the inner dialogue in this 16th verse of the Tao, but the main takeaway for our purposes is how important it is to learn how to shift away from that constant chatter.

Try thinking of the mind as a pond with different levels. The surface, which is a small percentage of the pond, is where all the disturbances are, and the mind is very much like that as well. On the pond, the turbulence of the waves, the leaves, the dirt, the wind, the constant freezing and thawing, the rain hitting it, the snow pelting it, and so on are all disturbances. In the mind, it's this constant chatter, this constant rumination.

If you drop a pebble through the pond of the mind, and it goes down a little bit below the surface, you'll find what we call "analysis." This picking things apart is essentially intellectual violence. The mind just below the surface is constantly doing this: *Why did he do that? Why did she do that? Why is this working that way?*

As you learn to be contemplative, you go a little deeper in the mind. The pebble drops below the level of analysis to what we call "synthesis." In synthesis, things are held together rather than torn apart. The mind sees the connection between things, and the illusion of your separateness is shattered. You see how everything is connected.

As the pebble drops a little farther, it goes to the place where all thoughts are removed, what we call "emptying the mind." You get very quiet. You get into "the gap," that space between your thoughts.

Ultimately, the pebble comes to rest in the Divine and perfect place that has many names, where God resides. Here is that Divineness that is within you. As it says in the Bible, "With God, all things are possible" (Matthew 19:26). Now, you tell me what that leaves out? It leaves out nothing. God's one and only voice is silence, so the greatest tribute you can give yourself is the space to hear it.

When you allow yourself to shut down your inner dialogue through the process of cultivating the witness and banishing doubt, you abandon the belief systems you've been taught by well-meaning people. It is here that your beliefs start to shift to knowings. You banish all doubt about your higher self and come to *know*.

That's the third key to higher awareness. It is about learning how to put more silence, space, and contemplation into your life, accepting less of the inner tumult that removes the peace and the harmony from it.

Here are a few suggestions for shutting down your inner dialogue:

— I recommend this affirmation, which I use quite frequently: *The more I listen, the more profound the silence becomes.*

— Try the following exercise, which uses the metaphor of the pebble dropping through the various levels of your mind. Note that you'll be doing it from the perspective of the witness, so you may want to reread that section before doing this visualization. You need to be able to observe while it's happening.

Visualize your mind as a pond, and see the disturbances at the surface, the chatter. Then see the analysis. See the pebble dropping to where you synthesize, and see the thoughts beginning to quiet. Witness the emptying of the mind. Finally, witness the pebble coming to this perfect, Divine field of all possibilities. When you get to that field, all you know is bliss. You will bring back from that experience solutions to the things that are so troubling to you. The solutions become very real because they are where the problems are. You do not look for the solution outside anymore. You are now facing a different way, inward, where you can directly tune in to the wisdom of your higher self.

— When you notice your mind becoming overly crowded with thoughts or going through inner turmoil, practice not focusing on anything for a few moments. Bring some stillness into the inner chatter. Tell yourself, *My mind is full of the disturbance of chatter and thoughts. I'm going to try to spend five minutes without any thoughts bombarding it.*

It's almost like you put a bubble around your mind. When a thought tries to penetrate that bubble, which is really the doing of the ego, it says, *Think me.* Then another one comes in and says, *No, think me! I'm really important.* So you give in. And your first thought is, *This is really silly.* Then another thought comes in: *You've got work to do.* Another one says, *You've got to get some groceries on the way home.* Another one says, *Yeah, and you've got to pay your bills.* Each one of them says, *Think me.* It's the ego trying to convince you that this is what you have to do.

So put a bubble around all that and let them bounce off. Use your breath as a means to keep your mind from chattering away ceaselessly. Your breath and your thinking go hand in hand. Take deep, long breaths in; and deep, long breaths out. As you concentrate on this, you'll find a peace coming over you.

You could also use your heartbeat like this, as a focal point for the witness. Or when you find your thoughts right below the surface in the analyzing level, think of a rose. As you replace the analyzing with the beauty of a rose, think about what Rabindranath Tagore, the great Indian poet, said: "Do we not carry a rose to our beloved because in it is already embodied a message, which unlike our language of words, cannot be analyzed." It just is. It needs no analyzing. Neither do you, and neither does your life.

— Another suggestion is that when you're at the synthesizing level, when you're feeling the beauty and unity of life, you may discover that you're entertaining thoughts of pleasure about enjoying the spiritual space. Let go of those thoughts too. You want to shut down *all* of this inner dialogue that muddies the way to the field of possibility. See, the ego enjoys convincing you that you're better than others because you're more spiritual. That's one of the big traps.

As you feel yourself becoming more spiritual, as you feel yourself becoming more awake, as you experience the authentic freedom of higher awareness, you might get the notion of *I truly am a little bit more spiritual than the other people I'm around,* or *My partner doesn't really know what path I'm on,* or the like. That's the ego trapping you into thinking that you are better or more special. You are not. Everyone is on their own place on life's path, and none of us are more special or better in the eyes of God. We are all extensions of that Divine, loving presence. We are not "better than." As you synthesize and see how all things are connected, don't let the ego convince you that this somehow makes you superior. It's a trap that the ego loves to get you in.

— In any moment of stress, go within and allow the pebble to drop, even if it's only for a few seconds. You can do this any time, any place. You can even do it in the middle of a busy meeting: Excuse yourself for a moment, go outside, and get quiet. See the pebble drop down, and let the calmness and serenity of your higher self take over. When you come back from that, you'll find yourself returning to the meeting with a clarity that you didn't have before, because you've allowed your higher self to run your life in that moment rather than your ego.

You're going to sever the connection between thoughts and outcomes by quieting the mind, and that stillness will bring you great joy. When the ego is silent, everything in the catalog of your personality that is associated with selfish desire begins to disappear. Things like loneliness, despair, illness, anger, fear, and worry are all part of that catalog of your personality and can be very loud—except when you get quiet and listen to your inner, higher voice.

— Finally, I recommend that you sign up for a martial arts class of some kind, something that teaches you about the energy of quieting down and allowing your body to function in its perfect, Divine order.

It's vitally important that you sever the connection between negative outcomes and the way you're thinking, and the three keys detailed here will indeed help you do that. There is a fourth key, however, which we'll take a close look at in the next chapter. Taken together, these keys to higher awareness will give you a power and freedom you never could have imagined.

CHAPTER 6

TAME THE EGO (THE FOURTH KEY)

The fourth key to higher awareness is so important that it requires its own chapter. It is "tame the ego," and it flows directly from the first three keys. After you banish the doubt, you learn to have a knowing rather than a belief about things. Then you are able to attain the perspective of the witness, noticing what's happening in a dispassionate way. In the process, you learn that cultivating the witness is best done in silence.

The ego works really hard at keeping you from that Divine place of a quiet mind, making you believe that there is nothing of value to you in silence. More than anything else, the ego is into self-preservation, and it will say things to you like, "I can't believe you're now allowing yourself to fall for all of this nonsense." "All of this nonsense" simply refers to your understanding that it is time to listen to your higher awareness. As you remove the doubt, cultivate the witness, and shut down the inner dialogue, you are preventing the ego from interfering in the daily decision-making of your life.

In this chapter, we'll learn some more about the ego, so we can clearly understand that which we need to tame.

SEVEN CHARACTERISTICS OF THE EGO

I have identified seven specific characteristics of the ego, which I will touch on briefly here and expand on later in the book:

1. The ego is your false self. It is your *idea of yourself,* and therefore not your true self. Your ego is not real; it is an illusion. It is something that you have come to believe in.

Your ego tries to convince you that you're something you're not. It wants you to believe that you are this body, so you have to make it better than other people's bodies, and you have to have more wealth and so on. This is false because your real self—which is eternal, changeless, and formless—doesn't care about any of those things.

2. It teaches separateness; that is, separate from God and from other people. Your ego says that you are distinct in all the world, and that uniqueness and separateness must be nurtured and protected at all times. You're constantly comparing yourself to other people or defending yourself from them. Your real self, however, knows that we are all one.

3. It convinces you of your specialness. The ego says you are not only separate from others, you are special too— you are better than others because of who you are and your background. You have to get rid of that idea because if you are special, it means that others aren't. We are all special in the eyes of God, so then why do we even need a term like *special?* It's just another fabrication of the ego.

4. It's always ready to be offended. The ego convinces you that anything that isn't the way you think it ought to be is a reason for you to be offended. It reinforces the belief that you are better than those people who are doing the offending and that God is doing work that you have to correct somehow. When you're offended, you get angry, and you fight and protect your specialness and separateness.

You have to learn to treat others the same way you would treat a jaguar who was trying to eat you. You wouldn't be offended by it. You would say, "I'd like to get out of its way, but I'm not offended by what it is." That's how you have to learn to be with everyone and everything in the world.

5. It is cowardly. I love this quote from Dr. Kenneth Wapnick, who was a wonderful teacher of *A Course in Miracles*:

> The ego is nothing more than a belief, and it is a belief in the reality of separation. The ego is the false self that seemingly came into being when we separated ourselves from God. Therefore, as long as we believe that the separation is real, the ego is in business. Once we believe that there's no separation, then the ego is finished. And cowardliness is a characteristic of the ego because the ego will do everything in its power to keep you believing in your separation from everyone else.

The ego operates on fear and cowardice. It's terrified of your getting to know the higher part of yourself, and it will do everything that it can to keep you from facing directly inward and tuning in to that power within. The ego is afraid of the celestial light that is within you, that inner knowing of bliss and peace, because your adherence to it will mean that the ego is no longer necessary in your life.

The cowardice of the ego is transformed by your inner light in the same way that a fear of the dark is transformed by turning on an outer light. Put another way, cowardly behavior is simply a symptom of great fear, and the antidote to fear is courage.

6. It thrives on consumption. The false self continually bombards you with the idea that you must have more in order to be happy. It pushes you toward comparing yourself to other people, to looking at all your acquisitions and saying, "I am better than others and more special because I have a newer car, a bigger house, nicer clothes, and a more attractive partner." It is always pushing you in the direction of consuming so that you can reinforce your separateness. As we've learned, such ideas are counterfeit, as authentic freedom never requires more.

7. And finally, the ego is insane. One of the definitions of *insanity* is "when someone believes themselves to be something they're not." Well, the ego always wants you to believe that you are this false self, which is separate and distinct in all ways, rather than something that is connected to and a part of a Divinity that it fears more than anything.

THERE IS NO SEPARATION

Despite what your ego insists, you are not separate from anyone. You do not have to be better than anyone, nor are you more special than anyone else in the world. You are that which is eternal and changeless. When you know that you are of spirit, that God is within you, you no longer have to prove yourself as someone who's better than others or gets offended by their actions.

I'm not saying you'll need to *conquer* the ego. There's no fighting here; this is not a war. Rather, you have to *tame* it by understanding what you are not. You are not your body, you are not your name, you are not your occupation, you are not any of those things that you have come to identify as who you are. You are in fact an eternal soul, a piece of Divine wisdom. When you come to know and believe in your true self rather than the idea of yourself, you learn to trust in the very wisdom that created you.

When you attain heightened spiritual awareness, what it does more than anything else is shatter the illusion of your separateness. As you see the horrible things that happen to people—all the struggles, all the poverty, all the hunger, all the things that I've spent much of my adult life working to eradicate—you understand that not only is our joy Divine and universal, but so too is our suffering. Everything that happens to one of us in life happens to all of us.

Therefore, it's critically important to release any sense of "us versus them." You can start by letting go of your ego's needs to be separate from others. Begin to view yourself as a member of the human family. The hand that gives gathers, so share with your neighbors and even strangers as if they were part of your own family—because they are.

Every time I travel to another country and go through customs, I think about how silly all this is. Somebody decided that this border belongs here and that border belongs there, and now here we are, hundreds or even thousands of years later, having to obtain passports and fill out forms in order to pass from one piece of land to another. Someone centuries ago decided it needed to be this way, and we've hung on to that mind-set. Of course we need to follow external laws and regulations, but internally we must know that we're all connected. We are all the same when it comes down to it, all part of one tribe called humanity.

Another way that you can continue to release this us-versus-them thinking is to note how many times you use the pronoun *I* in an hour. When you stop focusing on yourself as distinct from other people, you have more energy to extend your awareness to everyone. When you see yourself in terms of *we*, as part of the whole, then you open up space within you for the loving energy that's going to create the freedom of heightened awareness.

Because we are thought, and the universe is thought, the fastest vibration we have to either destroy or create is in our mind. Our mind is part of the universal mind, so creating unity and oneness is not actually difficult for us. But the ego tries very hard to keep us from realizing that power.

Your ego likes to keep you distracted from the messages of your higher consciousness, which affirm your ability to effect deep and lasting change. It keeps you absorbed in trivial matters, like the coffee you must have in the morning before you can function, the sweets that you need to munch on before you go to bed at night, or any number of daily diversions that you put so much energy into. Insignificant concerns, such as whether this report is filled out correctly, that deadline is being met, those people are following instructions, and so on, end up taking a great deal of your time.

Once you can let all this go, you can focus on the messages from your higher self. You'll discover that there is a profound, significant, and powerful drive that is at the core of your being. You have a deep need for your purpose, the reason you were put on this planet in the first place. You also know that purpose concerns unity; it has nothing to do with separateness or other shallow pursuits of the ego.

YOUR REAL SELF

Your ego tells you that you have to compete and consume. In order to prove yourself, you must have more toys. You need to accumulate more. You must achieve more. Your ego tells you that how good your body looks and how you smell and how much jewelry you have is important. There is a whole world of egos dealing with egos out there, everybody telling everybody how important they are. But you don't have to give in to that! You don't have to say, "Yes, but you should have heard what *I* did! Let me tell you."

Know that this self-importance has nothing to do with self-esteem. Self-esteem is a given. You don't have to question your esteem, your value, your confidence in who you are. You are a creation of God; you are Divine. It's just that God doesn't play favorites or make mistakes or think that anyone is special.

The less self-absorbed you are, the more freedom you have. When you're so hung up on everything having to be a certain way, your freedom is taken away from you. The ego promotes that sort of attachment, while the higher self is unattached to it.

It can be helpful to think of the ego like a shadow: When you go out into the light, you cast a shadow. The shadow, like your ego, is not real. You can't get hold of it. It's an illusion. Your higher self, of course, is what is real. It's wonderful to know your real self because then you don't live with the illusory shadow, which is always changing.

Similarly, you look at this packaging you're in, and every gray hair and wrinkle that appears is like a little notification that reminds you of your death. The ego wants you to believe that your body is where you should attach your primary identification. For the ego, the most embarrassing event in the world is death. But you know you are not this body; you are that which is observing it. Your real self is eternal and changeless.

Another great way of saying this is from the Bhagavad Gita: "You were never born; how can you die? You have never suffered change; how can you be changed? Unborn, eternal, immutable, immemorial. You do not die when the body dies." What a freeing notion it is when you identify with the part of you that is changeless and eternal rather than the body identification that the ego promotes so strongly.

I want to reinforce this point: the higher self is the real self; the ego is the shadow. That which is never changing, that which was never born, that which is eternal is the part of you that is actually processing this right now. It is so important that you remember this.

The more I get into this area of higher consciousness and heightened spiritual awareness, the more flabbergasted I become. It's just blowing me away. Knowing the real self, the God within, means that you're never alone. Everything you ever need is right there for you in abundance—and it keeps showing up.

I like to test it now. It's like, "All right, God. If You're really there, try this one on." I'll be in the process of writing something that is very much aligned with purpose, not being attached to whether people are going to like it, or my publisher is going to be happy with it, or it's going to be on the bestseller list, or I'm going to make money . . . all those things have left my life. Nowadays, I am focused on writing from my heart. I ask myself this question over and over again: *How may I get out of my own ego? How may I serve?* The answers unfailingly come to me.

When I write a book, I think about it for about a year, tossing the ideas around in my mind. When I'm ready to write, I leave my office and my home, but I stay close by. I'll get a large room and fill it with books: books that people have sent me, some I've been reading, a few I've heard about, those that publishers sent me for review, and all that. This process has emphasized for me that there are no accidents. Even if I think a book has nothing to do with me, it has part of consciousness in it. I can open up any book and find exactly what I've been looking for right there. So I surround myself with all sorts of things, and then I'll stop in the middle of writing and walk over and pick something up at random. I can trust that whatever I need will be right there for me.

If you can also get to the point where whatever shows up in your life can be processed by the higher part of yourself, then you will no longer be at the mercy of your ego—you'll be listening to your real self. In this place, amazing things will happen. When you let go and trust, miracles manifest.

CHAPTER 7

KNOW THAT WE'RE ALL ONE

Let's talk about cells for a moment. When there is harmony within one cell, the one next to it cooperates with that cell. It doesn't try to hurt it or destroy it; it is at peace. In this way, harmony and cooperation are the essence of life. When there is no ease or serenity or peace within a cell—when there is *dis-ease,* or disease—it gets aggressive and tries to harm the cell next to it. That diseased cell has no reference to the whole. And if something has no *reference* to the whole, it also has no *regard* for the whole.

For instance, we have many life-forms that make their home on and within us that might appear ugly if we looked at them under a microscope, but they have a reference to the whole. Be it the bugs in the lining of the stomach and in the intestine, in the toenails, or inside the nose, they all have a reference to the whole and work in conjunction or harmony.

In fact, while each of us thinks of ourselves as a singular unit, we are made up of a lot of life, a lot of different bacteria and so on that work together on and within us. We walk around all day long and think, *I'm an individual; I'm an island.* Yet without those millions of microscopic life-forms working together, we couldn't make it! If something were to come along inside our organisms that no longer had a reference to the whole, we'd be eliminated along with it. Disharmony, then, would be the thing that destroyed us.

Cancer can grow and influence other cells to become diseased when we don't have harmony within; consequently, it can destroy itself and the entire body along the way. A cancer in society operates in the same fashion. That is, when one individual—one "cell" who doesn't have ease within itself and has no reference to the whole of society—doesn't see itself as part of us, it can influence all those around it until it reaches a state where it destroys itself.

So the answer to a cancer, whether it's in a cell or in society, is to get harmony within. If you have harmony within you, then you will cooperate with the cell next to you, just like the cell in your body does—it's the same thing. In both cases, it is the answer to peace and to health.

This is all a mini-lesson in metaphysical philosophy. It's all relative—that's what Einstein taught us. And Nietzsche said, "All things being relative, what time does Munich stop at this train?" That'll give you something to think about.

But it *is* all relative. Is a cell in the body smaller or bigger than the cell that is you, this totality that is you? In an endless universe, a cell being bigger or smaller than you are is simply a question of context. Every part of it is as necessary and important as any other.

To think of it another way, the bug that is down in my toenail, which seems so distant from me, is still a part of me. We are all one. As we discussed in the last chapter, oneness and universalness is not mere speculation—we connect to it all. If all of us have harmony within us, and we're flowing with the universe, it can be the most powerful thing in the world.

EVERYONE IS CONNECTED AND NECESSARY

One day when I was running, I was thinking about how we're all one yet we're so stuck on our separateness. There was another runner about 30 yards ahead of me, and as I watched him, I thought, *How could it be that I am one with that person? I don't know his name. I don't know anything about him at all. How could there be any connection between us?* Suddenly, I had a really stunning realization that even though there was a distance between this runner and me, we were absolutely connected. I was reminded that all of us are, but we tend to look at things from a very limited perspective. Again, the ego loves to convince us of our separateness.

Here's something to try the next time you pull into a gas station and somebody is ahead of you, blocking the lane or parked in a place where you think you should be. Instead of getting upset, see them as being exactly where they need to be. Don't get angry; treat them with acceptance. Remember to always have an open heart. See your connection to this person instead of their separateness from you; treat them as if they were part of you, because they are!

Try to find other opportunities to practice this thought exercise, remembering that everybody out there is somehow, in some way, connected to you. Stop being antagonistic toward others. Think about how things would go if you got antagonistic toward the microbes that live inside your large intestine, telling them, "I'm going to do everything I can to get you guys out of there." That would kill you! You literally need that life. This is equally true, at a different level, for all of humanity. So start seeing everybody as part of you, necessary for your existence. Before long, you'll be feeling a strong sense of connection, just as I did with my fellow runner.

You'll understand all this when you leave this form that you're so attached to and go into another dimension—you'll clearly see that all of humanity is one. Imagine that you could see all of humanity represented as a jigsaw puzzle, but with a piece missing. Of course your eye would go right to what's lacking, noting that the puzzle cannot be complete without that piece. Well, you are one of the pieces of this puzzle called humanity, and if you are missing from it or not in harmony, then you make the whole incomplete. That's exactly how important you are as a person: you make humanity complete.

Science is proving what metaphysics has been saying for centuries. When you study life at the tiniest subatomic level, all the particles seem to be interconnected in some mysterious way. They're all sort of controlled by some force outside, some mystical thing, and they're all on purpose. There's nothing random about any of it. There's no happenstance in the universe.

I find this concept so intriguing. If every subatomic particle is on purpose and we're made out of those, then why wouldn't this apply to us? I remember being in New York City one day around 5:00 P.M. and seeing countless people come out from underneath the ground. It looked like an anthill. They had all just come off the subway and were all going someplace at the same time. I look back now and think they were all on purpose, like those subatomic particles.

Things like this appear random to us because our vision is so narrow; we tend to view everything from the limited perspective of our form. When you know that everything is on purpose, it stops you. You see everyone doing exactly what they're supposed to be doing. They're right where they belong, and you feel a blessed wave of acceptance wash over you.

ONLY LOVE TO GIVE

I almost always turn the things that used to upset me into love situations these days. For example, I came back to my car one day and found that a parking attendant was writing me a ticket for being approximately 30 seconds over the allotted time. My reaction to that 10 years ago would've been one of anger: "How dare you?!" I have since developed a kind of internal shield against the way others behave; it is on them, not me. I don't let other people's behavior own me any longer, since it's not me they're talking to but my role of rent-a-Wayne-Dyer.

This time, I walked over and started talking to the attendant. I engaged her in general, relatable chatter—for example, "Do you have any children?" and all that. She was halfway through the ticket, determined that she was going to keep writing it. I said, "If you have to write the ticket, it's all right. I don't have any problem with you doing your job. You're a very pleasant, nice person." With that, she tore up the ticket. Now, whether she would or wouldn't have given me a ticket would've been okay. My choice was to give love without being attached to any outcome.

Similarly, I often talk to people in service professions— particularly waitstaff, flight attendants, cab drivers, and the like—and I've found that the highest-functioning people in those professions are those who understand this concept: *People are not talking to me. They're talking to this role. So they're treating the role of server this way, and it has nothing to do with me.*

The way you get harmony within you is through your thinking. So if someone sends you hate, but you have only love inside, then love is all you'll have to give away. Furthermore, your giving will help diffuse the hate. It's really hard to hate somebody who sends you back love. It's hard to fight with somebody who doesn't want to fight. I don't know if you've ever tried to argue with somebody who refuses to argue with you, who's just not interested, who isn't going to play your game. You have to learn how to do that with children all the time, because they're constantly trying to corner you or get you trapped into their illogic. And once you buy into it, you're completely sucked in.

So my server friends act at the highest levels toward others. That is, when they're sent anguish, hatred, and bitterness, they send back love because that's all they have inside to send away. They do the same thing with their bosses. They have gotten to the point where they understand, *These people are difficult, behaving in foolish and obnoxious ways, but that has nothing to do with me. That's not mine in any way. I am going to send them back love.*

As you become totally awake, with your heightened spiritual awareness, you find yourself less and less consumed with how other people treat you. If it gets too bad or difficult for you, you move on without bitterness. You don't say, "He shouldn't be acting this way," or She's no good," or whatever. You just move away, even if you can only do it in your mind. The way that you process all this is really the key.

You can take almost the worst of situations, and if all you have to give away is harmony because that's all that you are, you can turn the situation into something positive very quickly. Especially if you're focused on the big picture, not attached to being upset or angry at the way that this person is treating you. You understand, *This is not really me that they're treating this way. Because the real me, the very essence of who I am, is not this body that they're talking to. It's how I choose to think. It's my thoughts, and they can never have that.*

What also happens is you begin to avoid conflict and confrontation altogether. You may have been taught that you have to prove that you can "deal with" those who challenge you. Well, the more awake and aware you get, the more you realize that conflict is a violation of harmony. You realize that if you participate in it, you become part of the problem rather than part of the solution. It gets easier to avoid conflict and confrontation when you don't have to be right anymore, when you see other people for where they are on life's path and you let them be there. If they want to be upset because they're stuck in traffic or their remote control isn't working right now, then that's absolutely fine.

I do this with my children all the time. They get an emotional attachment to whether this person calls, or whether they have to do the dishes, or any number of things; I don't even talk about it anymore. They know what their responsibilities are. I think, *I'm not going to join you. I'm simply not going to get seduced into having this kind of discussion,* and I move away from it.

At first, it's like you're acting—there is an aspect of "fake it till you make it." But after a while, it becomes second nature. Discord isn't in your life any longer; you don't even notice it. You don't have to be a wimp or be pushed around. You don't need to have anybody victimizing you at all. You just refuse to participate in anything that's going to drag you down. You know you don't have to engage in order to prove that you're better than somebody else. That wouldn't make you right, and it wouldn't make them wrong. When you understand where other people are, you don't need to be drawn into conflict at all. You can simply move on.

If enough human beings shied away from disharmony—if we agreed that it wasn't going to be a part of our lives anymore— imagine how much war and conflict we could eliminate.

LET GO OF JUDGMENT

Each and every one of us is part of the perfection of the universe. We are all on the same path, but each of us is on different places along that path. Once you understand this, it makes harmony that much easier.

I heard an interview recently in which the hosts were putting down rock music as being uncivilized or barbaric. The fellow being interviewed was a classical musician who said, "When I was much younger, I loved rock. I would play that stuff real loud, and it would drive my family crazy. Then I moved into ballads and things like that, and I had very little to do with rock 'n' roll. Now, of course, I compose classical music." Then he said, "I don't like to put down any type of music. I know that I needed to be at each one of the places I was along the path in order to be here." This talented artist was trying to explain that there is no need to think of someone as wrong, improper, or uncivilized just because they make a particular choice such as playing the kind of music you don't like.

Judgment is the mark of the ego, and you must work to get it out of you completely. After all, when you judge another person, you don't define them; you define *yourself.* If you're going to try to understand others in your life, you have to understand that wherever they are on the path of life is where they have to be in order to get to the next place. See them not so much as where you think they should be but where they are, knowing that where they are is absolutely necessary. Don't judge any of it; work on accepting it.

Not only is this very sensible when relating to other people, it also applies to yourself. When it comes to the things you're doing that aren't working for you—the constant seeking of approval, the depression you may be going through, the controlling relationships you're drawn to, the pursuit of stuff in order to simply have it, and so forth—don't judge yourself and say, "I shouldn't be doing this." There's no room for judgment in a person who is truly awake and aware.

Once you get to that point, you'll catch yourself all the time. I know I do: I'll be talking to someone and say, "Well, not to be judgmental, but . . . ," and then I proceed to be judgmental about this thing that I don't like in the news or whatever it is. When that happens, I don't stop myself and say, "I shouldn't be doing this." Instead, I accept that I still have some judgmental stuff in me. I know that as long as I'm judging other people, I'm defining me, not them. Then the next time I'm less inclined to do that, and the next time I'm even less inclined, and so on.

Eventually you get to the point where you can see people's behavior for what it is. You don't have to like it, you don't have to tell yourself that they have a right to hurt others, or anything like that. *You just stop judging it.* You see them for where they are on the path, and then you do the same thing to yourself. You see where you are, and then you realize that everything you're doing is necessary to get you to the next step and beyond. You'll see yourself as having to go through all this in order to get past it, to get to the point where your higher self is in charge rather than your ego.

EVERYONE IS A TEACHER

I travel all over the world, and I know that every person I encounter has something to teach me—it may be to be a little more generous and give a little more, or it may be to just give a smile or to be loving, but there is a lesson there.

In fact, I have a very strong belief that everyone who comes into our lives, from the stranger sitting next to us on the bus to our family members, is a teacher. The key is to take the point of view of the student, eager to learn what they have to teach us. When you look at it that way, taking away some of your snobby attitudes, and your holier-than-thou, better-than-somebody-else, ego-driven kind of thinking, you open yourself up to frequent guidance from the universe.

Take that little old lady who's driving in front of you at 20 miles an hour in her 1976 cream-colored Cadillac, of which she can hardly see over the steering wheel. Well, she signed an oath that she will drive around aimlessly, testing your ability to effectively deal with her. She is a gift from God. You need to stop being mad at her for being who she is and what she's about and understand that she's exactly where she's supposed to be. She's there to teach you a very important lesson. In that moment that you're about to get angry and speed around her (and maybe even have a car accident), that's the moment she teaches you the lesson: *You have to slow down. Relax.*

There's an old saying that you will not be punished *for* your anger; you will be punished *by* your anger. That makes a lot of sense to me. It isn't like there's going to be a Judgment Day in which somebody's going to tally up how many times you were angry and give you points or whatever. Instead, what happens is that you find yourself living with that anger.

When you expect the world to be the way you want it to be instead of honoring it and celebrating it the way it is, you will be punished by your anger. Anger, hatred, and bitterness—as well as all the stuff that comes out of you in the name of getting somebody else to change or not liking the way the world is—becomes what you're constantly marinating in. It is something that you live with all the time, so that's all you have to give away. It intensifies the stress that you're living with, and it raises your heart rate and creates all kinds of physical maladies.

So don't give anyone else control over the Divine part of you, the intelligence that suffuses your form and constitutes your entire humanity. Think of yourself as connected to and part of it all, rather than someone who is being victimized. Remember, everything that happens is part of the perfection of the Divine plan.

That's a very nice place to get to. It doesn't take away your ability to make choices; it takes away your wanting the world to be as you think it should be instead of as it is. It's all in how you perceive things and choose to process them. If you see everybody as a teacher, then you'll always be open to the universe's education.

Even those who cause us deep anger and frustration and might be termed "petty tyrants" can bring us invaluable lessons. Society has handed us this idea that they are bad, so we should have hatred toward them or, at the very least, ignore them. As we've learned, however, everyone or everything that comes our way has some kind of purpose. We can't be awake beings with heightened spiritual awareness or be authentically free if we believe that only the things that we like and approve of are part of the Divine plan. No, *everything* is part of the Divine plan, period. We don't have to like or understand it in order for it to be part of Divinity.

My father was a petty tyrant, yet he influenced me in dramatic ways. I call him my greatest teacher, as it was the act of forgiving him that brought me to a higher level of awareness. I can also think of many of the people whose lives I have touched as a therapist and as a friend, and see that the person they have a great deal of enmity and anger toward was one of the greatest teachers of *their* lives.

If you look at the times when you have moved to a higher spiritual place in your life, you'll often find that it was preceded by some kind of a fall, such as a divorce, a bankruptcy, or an unexplained illness. This is true not only for each one of us individually but also for us collectively. Very often the difficulties and conflicts that nations go through teach us how to transcend that level of thinking for resolving our disputes.

Every single fall of your life, and every single petty tyrant that has ever showed up, has really been an opportunity for you to advance spiritually. Believe it or not, the ego is terrified of your fall—it would rather that you have a nice, steady stream of misery. It doesn't want you to have a major crisis. It doesn't want you to have a heart attack. It doesn't want you to have a divorce. Your ego knows that when you fall, that's when you tend to find God. That's when you go to the higher part of yourself, and the ego is terrified of either the higher self or of God being a part of your life.

With this new perspective, I'm sure that if you look back you can see how every fall you've experienced has actually been an energy propeller to get you to a higher level of awareness. Therefore, I suggest that when you encounter a petty tyrant in your life now, instead of viewing them as someone to be ignored or angry at, ask, *What is this doing for me now so that I generate energy to move me along spiritually?* That's a great ancient teaching, and it applies in all of our lives.

All of the beliefs that I've talked about in this chapter are huge. The notions that you are separate, you are important, you are distinct, you need to be offended, you have to consume, you have to be in comparison to other people, are all ideas that the false self has used. Such messages have been absorbed collectively in our society as well: The world ego keeps people from knowing the celestial light by focusing whole cultures on what makes us separate from each other, so we can build weapons to destroy each other and therefore stay in constant states of conflict. It's done at the collective level; it's done on the individual level. But these are things that we can all transcend.

When you shift to a mind-set that we are all one—and know the peace, bliss, and joy of harmony that comes with this—you will perform at higher and higher levels. Again, the irony is that you'll have all you need, coming to you in the amount that is sufficient to take care of you, yet you will not be attached to anything considered valuable in the world of form. When you're unconcerned about being special and separate, genuine success will be yours.

CHAPTER 8

SURRENDER AND GO WITH THE FLOW

There is a fundamental understanding that comes with awakening, which is that there is an order to things and each of us is part of this order. In the Hindu tradition, this is known as *dharma*. It refers to our duty, or how we fit into this perfect order, the Divine plan.

Here's a great story that illustrates this concept. A sage was seated beside a river and noticed a scorpion that had fallen in. He reached down and rescued it, only to be stung. Sometime later, he saw the scorpion thrashing about in the water again. Once more, he reached down and rescued it, and once more he was stung.

A bystander observing all this exclaimed, "Holy one, why do you keep doing that?! Don't you see that the wretched creature will only sting you in return?"

"Of course," the sage replied. "It is the dharma of a scorpion to sting. But it is the dharma of a human being to save."

Understanding the order of things means that you don't suspend your own dharma—your place in this order, or your purpose as a human being—in order to fit in with somebody or something else's behavior or dharma. You always know what you're about, that this fundamental order is there, and that who you are and everything that happens to you is all part of the Divine plan of the universe.

THE PLACE OF TRUST AND SERENITY

Before I speak to an audience, I like to take the time to get centered rather than thinking about whether people are going to like what I have to say. I've shifted to visualizing them loving what I'm doing and knowing that it's going to work. I trust in the Divineness that I am, not concerned with this package I'm in that is wearing away. I know that I am in harmony with the intelligence that is suffusing me, which some call God, some call spirit, some call soul, and some call consciousness. It really doesn't matter what we label it. This concept of understanding that universal intelligence is a part of our consciousness is not only for mystics; it's not something for people to go contemplate in caves. It's for every one of us in the practice of our daily lives, in whatever business we're in.

I know that things are going to work out for me and that the power of who I am is not in this body. Once I started putting myself in this place of trust, all I can say is that my speaking to audiences has never been better. I'm as relaxed and authentic and enthusiastic about what I'm doing as I ever was, but I tend to have fewer notes in front of me. In fact, I often don't have any. I've surrendered to an understanding that as long as what I'm about is helping to improve the quality of life for others, then universal intelligence will take over and protect me from walking onstage and going blank. I know I won't stumble and mumble, get lost and not know what I'm doing, fall down, or whatever one fears might happen when speaking in public. That faith has paid off, as I've had some incredible audience experiences.

Once you have this knowing that you are on target in your life, in the service of others, you'll understand the serenity that I'm talking about. This serenity isn't solely in you; it's in the whole universe. That's what you surrender to. Any anxiety, worry, or fear—that you're not going to have "success," you're not going to perform, you're not going to achieve, or you're not going to accumulate—are not the operating values in your life anymore. I'm not saying that those things won't be in your life at all, but they simply won't be the primary motivators for you any longer.

All the things I do, from writing and speaking to the appearances I make in the media, are motivated by a genuine internal desire to bring about more stability and peace and harmony in the world for people in some way. With that knowing, life just seems to flow, and everything seems to work a lot better for me than it once did.

You might be saying, "Yeah, okay. You're Wayne Dyer, and you've got all this validation and prosperity, so it's easy for you to say. But what about me? I'm trying to sell shoes for a living." Well, I believe that the same principle applies, no matter what position you find yourself in. Surrendering to the Divine within you is going to help, no matter what.

THE PEOPLE BUSINESS

Take a second to ask yourself, *What am I doing? What am I about? Is my life focused on trying to accumulate a lot of stuff?* If it is, you're going to feel a strong sense of frustration almost all the time because you'll be suffering from the ego's disease of having to get more.

If you think about what you're doing in your life, the ultimate bottom line is: Are you or are you not helping to improve the quality of life for another human being? If you're selling shoes, then look to see how those shoes are improving the quality of your customers' lives in some way—how they think about themselves, how their feet are protected, or what have you. Whatever it is that we're doing, all of us are in the people business in one way or another. So it really helps to have this knowing of *The focus of my life isn't how much money I'm going to get, or what kind of awards I'm going to receive, or how I'm going to climb this ladder of success within my corporation. My motivation is simply to serve others.*

I get hundreds of letters every week, and I try to answer as many as I can. I remember a lady wrote me years ago to say: "At a speech you gave before the American Association of Counseling and Development in Los Angeles, you mentioned an essay by Abraham Maslow called 'The Whole Man.' I have searched high and low for that. Can you tell me where I can get it?"

Keep in mind that this was before widespread access to the Internet or e-mail. After I read her letter, I thought, *Sure, I could send her a little note and say, "This is where you can find it," but I'd rather send her the article.* I knew this particular article was in a book in my library, but I wasn't quite sure where. I looked all over the place until I finally found it. Then I asked my secretary to copy the article, which was about 70 pages. Again, this was years ago, so it was a bit of an undertaking. I wrote back to the lady and said, "Instead of telling you where to find it, I am sending you a copy of the article." I sent it along with one of my own books.

Now, I had no idea who this woman was other than someone who worked for a mental health institution in New York. After I put the package in the mail, I had a brief moment of doubt. But then I stopped myself and remembered that I was on the right path, that I wasn't doing this to sell her anything, persuade her that I was this wonderful altruistic person, or anything like that. I had surrendered to what I am about. Rather than thinking about what this gesture would do for me, I did it because I felt it was the right thing to do. I did it simply for the reason that it would help to improve her quality of life in some way. I believed it to be a loving, decent, kind thing to do, and hopefully it made things easier for her.

Having said that, I also knew that many terrific things would come about as a result of that one act. She would tell other people about it, and they would go out and do kind things for others. The goodwill would keep circulating, on and on, until the kindness returned back to me. I feel this is how we create a better world. I consider my own life, as I live it every day, to be a work of art in progress. Furthermore, the work of art that is my life is one of serving more, giving more, making more of a difference, and being more in harmony.

The state of the world is really nothing more than a reflection of our state of mind. So my state of mind about my world reflects my belief that there is a higher consciousness that is a part of who I am. That God force, or love force, is what I am about, what I'm here for. The more I find myself acting in accordance with the Divine, the more wonderful things happen to me.

For example, I've released my attachment to money in favor of trusting in abundance. It is now unusual for me to go to my mailbox and *not* find money that somebody has sent me. Oftentimes, it's from people who believe in the principle of tithing, or seed money; that is, if they read or hear something that they find benefit or value in, they send support to that person. These folks seem to live by a code of generosity and supporting people and causes they believe in. So I get checks like this in the mail all the time.

As I discussed earlier in the book, my mind-set has shifted from being surprised by abundance or miracles to expecting them. I've noticed as well that in releasing my attachment to money, I've let go of my need to have a bargain. That's a real growth for me, because I used to believe that if I couldn't get a bargain, then I shouldn't buy something at all.

While I certainly never ask to be sent money like this, I am sure to recirculate the funds I receive. Every time I get a check, I think, *Wow, somebody sent me some money, but it isn't for me. It's for the work that I'm doing, so what can I do with it?* I might give it to Amnesty International to help free prisoners of conscience around the world. Or I'll buy books and audio programs to donate to libraries, prisons, or other centers that need the material. Sometimes I'll see a story in the news about somebody who's struggling in some way or another, and I'll take that money and channel it toward them. It becomes like this magnificent circle, facilitated by a bunch of us helping each other.

Again, I'd like to stress that every one of us is in the people business. Somehow, in some way, the basic bottom line for each of us is to improve the quality of life for some other human being. So if we know that that's the business we're in, then we can apply this concept globally. World peace comes about through inner peace within each individual. Therefore, if we've got a whole world full of people who are peaceful, then we've got world peace. But if we've got a world full of some individuals who are peaceful and a whole bunch more who are full of anger, dissension, fear, mistrust, and so on, then we've got world disorder.

The same is true in any organization—it all starts with getting your own act together. Trying to get ahead of the next guy should never be your focus, because that's not what the people business is about. It's about improving life for all people. When you improve your own life first, all you'll have to give away is quality of life. If you do that, and you're giving away quality in every interaction that you have, you will be the kind of person whom other people want to be around.

When you become this type of person, you'll be more effective at your job because people want to be around you. Walk into any automobile dealership, for instance, and you can easily find somebody whom no one wants to be around. That person usually doesn't sell very many cars, whereas the person you want to be around tends to be very successful.

If you're feeling uninspired in your organization, however, the universe is sending you a message: *Move along.* Don't tell yourself that you're stuck. Don't become consumed with the posturing and the awards that go with your position, the opinions of other people, and other hallmarks of the ego. If your sole and total focus is on living the life you've imagined, wonderful things will happen.

You've got to trust that you'll know when it's time to make a change. If you don't, the universe will tell you— you'll get the signal in some way, and you will indeed move along. If you continue to stay where you don't belong, the universe will start making you deteriorate: You might get sick or have an accident. Whatever the signal is, it will indicate that things aren't working right for you, and you'll know it. But you have got to pay attention to the messages of the universe.

Let me remind you that one of the hallmarks of ego is fear. You must trust in the wisdom of your higher self, which knows that you can't ever make a mistake—there *are* no mistakes, as this is a perfect place. Everything is all working perfectly, and so are you.

KEEP IT FLOWING

In a society that has become almost obsessed with upward mobility, our possessions, and the accumulation of *more*, it's important to ask why: What are we planning to do with all this stuff?

Remember, you can't own anything—ever. You show up on this planet with nothing, and you leave the same way. I have a suit in which I have cut out all the pockets, and every time I open my closet, I see this funny-looking suit there with its holes and slashes. If anyone else sees it, they'll ask, "What in the world is that?" I'll respond, "That's to remind me that the last suit you wear doesn't need any pockets." It's a reminder that none of us is taking anything with us from the world of form.

As you've learned, the relationships you're in can only be experienced or processed through thought. You can't be your spouse or your children, and they can't be you. You can only process the experience of each other through thought. You can never get hold of them; they can never get hold of you. The illusion is that you have them, or that they have you, and you don't at all.

It's the same with your stuff: you don't own it; it owns you. As long as you "need" possessions and feel incomplete if you don't—if you don't have the fancy car, if you don't have the right house in the right part of town, if you don't have jewels on your fingers, and so on—that's a sign that you feel something must be lacking in your life. In this position of *I'm incomplete*, you're sure that your completeness will be fulfilled through material things. You get some diamonds, and then you say to yourself, *That should make me happy*, but it doesn't because possessions are just an illusion. Yet you think, *Maybe if I get bigger diamonds, or a better car, or . . .* You're constantly at the mercy of the ego's disease of more. Needing to have all the things that you accumulate and collect and hang on to and so on makes you a victim of those things. The irony is that the less you need, the more you'll get.

The totally awake person operates with heightened spiritual awareness, understanding that more is less and less is more. All of us are here temporarily. We're part of this dream, and for a very short time. We accumulate a certain amount of things while we're here, but we have no need for them when we leave this world of form. So fiercely clinging to things makes no sense. What does make sense is relaxing that grip, letting go of what we know we don't need so that we can make room for what we *do* need.

Everything in the universe flows, but the strongest things are those that flow the best. If you take water and a rock and put them together, which one is going to triumph over the other? The water will always wear away the rock. Yet if you try to reach in and get a handful of this stuff that is so powerful that it can wear away rock in practically no time at all, you will find that the tighter you squeeze, the less you get in your hand. You have to put your hand in the water and relax it, and only then can you experience the water. You can never hold on to it.

"Go with the flow" might be a clichéd saying, but there's a lot of meaning to that. It means you're not fighting anything; you're allowing it to happen. *Allowing* is another word for *surrender*. You must allow yourself to trust the Divine. Surrender and become unattached to how things turn out, even though this can be very difficult.

A good analogy for being detached from the things that we think are so important to us is to think of a symphony.

We're listening to the music, but we can never hear the whole symphony at one time. We can only hear it a moment at a time—we hear one note, then we hear another note, and then we hear another. That whole individual, step-by-step process, the flowing with it, the going with just one note, with whatever is happening, is what constitutes the experience called "symphony" and the appreciation of music. We don't sit back and say, "No, this note doesn't count. None of that counts. I want to hear the whole thing at once." We take each moment that comes and experience it, and we experience the next one, and so on.

It's silly to think of being able to appreciate music without being able to hear each individual note as it comes along. That's also how life is. It's absurd to become attached to the notion that we have to consume it all or have so many things.

Here's a great exercise in not being attached: Go through your house and the closets, gather up all the toys that your children don't use anymore, and give them away. Have the kids participate in this as well. Next, gather all the clothes that you haven't worn in the last 18 months. If you haven't worn it for a year and a half, it's no longer yours. We've already established that you can't own anything anyway—you come in naked and you leave that way. So send these clothes on to somebody else. Then go out to your garage, and collect everything that you've been so busy holding on to but not using. Give it away too. There's somebody else out there who can use all that stuff. Get it recirculating. Keep it flowing. Keep it moving.

Know that everything you feel you have to have owns you, which means you don't own yourself. To that end, many people can't leave where they're living right now because they don't know what to do with all the stuff they're hanging on to. They say, "I have too much here. I can't leave!"

This causes them to miss opportunities because they can't hear the messages the universe is sending them.

When you're not attached to things, they can't own you any longer. Then you'll find that you're less attached to ideas that no longer work in your life either. In the process, you'll open yourself up to so many positive experiences. What you once viewed as just happenstance or a coincidence shows up in your life in numerous ways now that you're really experiencing the awakened life. Again, the less attached you are, the more the universe will send your way. If you give away more of whatever you're getting, it all keeps moving and flowing, and your life improves beyond measure.

STRIVING VS. ARRIVING

Acceptance and being happy with where you are in life is not something Western society tends to teach. In fact, it can seem like you're programmed to go after something else from day one. It's like you're trained to think, *When I get out of this playpen, I'll have the whole room. Oh, get me out of here.* Then you get out of the playpen and into the room, and you think, *I'd like to go into the next room, but they've got one of those barriers across the hall. I've got to get past that gate that they put there. Then maybe I can get into the cupboards and have fun with the pots and pans. That'll be when I arrive.* Then it's like, *Maybe I can go out into the yard,* so the yard becomes the goal. Then you get out of the yard, and the goal is the block. Then there's a street to cross. There is always a "next."

You finally get into school, and all you can think about is getting out. What I remember about elementary school is lines. I hated lines and seeking permission. For five years, you've peed whenever you felt like it but now, all of a sudden, you have to ask permission. It's like, *Let me out of here. I don't want to ask permission to pee anymore.* Then you're going to geography class, and you have to stand in line. Why in the world do they do this? The lines don't move; you just stand there waiting. I guess if it moved, it wouldn't be a line—it would be a parade, wouldn't it?

Anyway, all you can think about is junior high—you know that when you get there, you'll get out of lines. But then you find out that this is not the place to be either. You realize, *They don't treat us like adults at all. We have to take whatever courses they give us, and we're always told to stop touching each other. Or, "Sit up." Or, "Quiet. No talking."*

Then your goal shifts again. It's like, *When I get to high school, that will be* it. *Life will be complete.* You get to high school, but then you realize you're a lowly little freshman. Even the word sounds yucky, so you bypass it. You think, *All right, I'll put up with this because next year I'll be a senior underclassman.* (You call yourself this as a euphemism for a sophomore.) You're telling yourself, *I want to get in the 10th grade because then I can learn to drive.* Nothing in the world counts now except getting a driver's license. Life is about nothing else when you're 14 and 15, just striving toward getting a driver's license. That's all there is . . . until you start thinking about dating. *Wow. When I can date, boy, that's when my life will be complete.*

Then it's like, *When I get out of high school, it'll be so great that I won't have to be told what to do.* Finally, you work hard and get out of high school, but there's no marching band. There's a ceremony and maybe a little party—but then you've got to face life. You say to yourself, *Well, maybe my life will start when I go to college. Surely that will be it.* Then you go through college, thinking, *No. This is not it at all. It's more of the same—just studying. Sure, I get to pick the classes I want, but it's the same old stuff.*

You get out of college. *They tell me when you get married, that's when your life really begins. That's when it's great, so I'll get married.* Then you find out that the partner you picked out makes funny noises that he or she never made before. It's just too much. You think, *All right. Marriage may not be it, but they tell me when you have a child, that makes you complete with the universe. I guess I'm not really a person yet—I'm sort of an apprentice person. But when I have that child, that's when I'll be complete.*

Then maybe you think, *They tell me that life gets going when you finally get that divorce. They say that divorce is the thing that really makes your life. My spouse drags me down all the time, so as soon as I get marriage out of my life, that'll do it.* Or maybe you focus on geography: *How did I get here anyway? My great-great-grandparents landed in this town, and I'm still here. What the hell am I doing here? That's it. I'll go to Hawaii. By the time I get to Hawaii,* then *I'll be complete.*

It's kind of endless: *Maybe when I get a new job, that'll be it.* Or, *They tell me when you get the promotion, that's the thing that really makes your life start.* Or, *What I've heard is that as soon as you retire, that's when life really gets going.* Then you retire, and you hear people talking about the good old days. But they never had a "good old day" in their whole life, because they were always postponing and had an aversion to now.

There aren't many people who understand what Carly Simon said, that *these* are the good old days. That's because everything you do is done in the present moment. A person who's always goal setting, thinking about the future, and concerned with what things are going to be like is doomed to eternal frustration rather than an appreciation of anything. They're constantly striving, never arriving.

LET GO OF BEING BEST—SIMPLY *BE*

Virtually everyone we've ever known has told us that in order to be successful, we must have goals. This is one of those aphorisms that guide our lives, the whole idea that if we don't know where we're going, then how will we know when we get there?

There are, in fact, other ways of learning other than to have goals. There's a word in Sanskrit, *satori,* and it speaks to the idea that when the student is ready, the teachers will appear. So in moments of insight, you can shift around things that you've spent a lifetime accumulating. You just have to be ready.

I can hear the doubts, because the importance of goals has been pounded into your head for your whole life. I'm not here to get in an argument nor to make anybody wrong who believes in these things strongly. All I'm suggesting is that you can have satori, an instant moment of shifting around, when you are ready and willing. Also, God works in very mysterious ways. If you have this readiness, you say, "I'm going to turn this whole problem or struggle over, and I know that the universe knows what it's doing. I'm going to surrender and allow the organizing Divinity that is a part of everything to work through me. I know that I'll be guided, and I'm not alone." The moment that you have that awareness, then goals don't seem to be nearly as significant or as important.

If you feel like you have to have everything all planned out in your life, with goals set up all along the way, you'll miss countless opportunities. There's an old saying that says, "If you really want to make God laugh, tell Him your plans." When you let go and let God, when you stop this insistence that you have to have everything planned out, then you will experience heightened spiritual awareness. Again, shift your focus from striving to arriving.

Another belief that most of us have hung on to for most of our lives—because, as you'll recall, it's been handed to us by well-meaning folks—is that we always have to do our best. I hear this almost every single day, from motivational speakers to athletes: "I have to do my best." I'd like to challenge that. You don't have to be perpetually performing and doing things at the top level. As a matter of fact, the idea that things always have to be done perfectly is very often what will keep you from achieving anything at all.

I was a doctoral advisor after I received my own doctorate, and I can remember having many students who would go through all the coursework but then couldn't write their dissertation because they "couldn't get it right." I'd say, "Look, you don't have to do your best at this thing. But you've got to get it done if you ever want to be able to have your doctorate." Like those students, if you're preoccupied with perfectionism, it will turn into paralysis in the end, because you won't be able to accomplish anything. Get rid of that whole idea of best and just do.

I suggest that you replace the idea that you always have to do your best at everything with this: *There's going to be a few things that I do very well—it may even be my best. But when it comes to the rest of the things I do in my life, I'm not going to worry about my best and instead simply enjoy them.* Remember to take that pressure off of your children as well, because it's far more important for them to do and enjoy and be at peace and in harmony than it is to live with all of the illness-producing stress that comes from constantly being told that you always have to do your best.

Your "best" is really a notion that the ego keeps promoting in order to keep you away from the higher part of yourself, which says, "You don't have to beat anybody. You don't have to do achieve. You don't have to perform. You simply have to *be:* Be at peace. Be at joy. Be at bliss." When you operate from this place, you will be unattached to the outcome of whatever it is you do. You'll be in process. You'll be enjoying the whole journey, rather than seeking out all these destinations that others have imposed on you.

One of the fundamental problems is that people want the world to be different than it is. Contrary to what you've heard, the world is a perfect place. There's no anxiety in it. There's no depression in it. There's no stress in it. There's only anxious thinking. There's only stressful thinking. There's only angry thoughts. There's no anger in the world.

You are also part of that perfect world; your perfection is in your own creation. You could never be a mistake. So once you surrender to your higher self and replace the ego's messages with the serenity and peace I've been talking about, you won't even know how to be victimized anymore. You will be in the universe's flow. You won't need to get there; you'll be living it.

CHAPTER 9

HARNESS THE POWER OF VISUALIZATION

When you are imbued with inner peace or serenity and are on the side of order, disorder is impossible for you. You no longer see yourself as a hapless victim. You see the intelligence behind everything, and this motivates you to seek solutions where others can only see impossible problems.

Here's an example of what I'm talking about. A while ago, I caught a flight from Fort Lauderdale to Chicago. I got on the airplane at one o'clock in the afternoon, we took off and flew for 30 minutes, and then we were informed that we were going to have to land in Miami. Apparently, they couldn't retract the landing gear, which was stuck in the down position. The airline staff was trying to convince us that there was no emergency, that those ambulances we saw in Miami were standing by in case anybody fainted while they watched us land, that the foam out there on the runways was so they could see if their foam equipment worked.

There was, in fact, some emergency. And there were lots of interesting reactions from the people around me on the plane. There were a lot of ashen looks, and a lot of very scared people—one couple even jumped up and screamed. But I didn't feel any of that. I saw myself being okay. It wasn't that I tried hard not to be fearful; it was that inside of me, something had replaced that fear. The serenity within assured me that everything was all right, and I was fine.

I chose to be effective, using my mind in a situation where other people might choose to panic. I calmed down the guy next to me. I looked around to see where the emergency exits were. I elected to be conscious, to be intelligent, and to think of survival. I wasn't the least bit afraid, yet I know I would have been in such a circumstance at an earlier time in my life. That potential for fear has been replaced now by peace and fulfillment as well as the knowing that when it's my turn, it's my turn, and that's okay. I know I'm not my form, so I'm not afraid of leaving it when the time comes.

Everything turned out to be fine on my flight, except now 192 people who were on this plane had to figure out what to do next. You see, the first thing they did once we landed safely was announce the following: No one would be getting a seat out of Florida because all the airlines were full. We'd probably have to be stuck in the airport while they figured out what to do. And no, they weren't going to put us up in a hotel.

Again, I watched the people around me. A minute ago, they were worried about whether or not they were going to live. Now they were relieved that they were alive, but they were also angry because of this additional information. It was like the airline was throwing every negative thing they could think of at us!

I believe in looking for solutions, never problems. So when the plane landed and they gave us that negative message, I knew they weren't talking to me. I saw myself in Chicago. I had a speech to give the next morning, and there were a lot of people depending on me to be there. I knew I'd be there, as opposed to the 191 other people who didn't believe they would be in Chicago and were acting that way. They were angry, they were upset, they were yelling at the airline personnel, they were letting their blood pressure get out of control—but they weren't actually *doing* anything.

As soon as we deplaned, I called my secretary in Fort Lauderdale and said, "Please make sure I have a seat on a plane. No matter what it costs or the inconvenience may be, get me a seat." When I called her back in 15 minutes, she told me that she was able to get me a seat on another airline. It turned out that somebody had canceled right before she called, and I was able to get that seat. Out of 192 people, I believe I was the only one who made it to Chicago that day. It didn't happen because I'm smarter or better than everybody else. Instead, I looked for solutions rather than problems because I refused to be victimized by the ego's need to be angry and right.

What this example shows is that when you are able to visualize yourself doing something, it becomes automatic for you to act on that visualization, or that image. You are then able to make the most incredible things happen.

TURNING YOUR VISION INTO REALITY

When you get an image in your mind of something you want, and you act on that image, it becomes what you are. An image is nothing more than a thought, and you know that as you think, so shall you be. The image is something that you will begin acting on, treating yourself as if you already are what you're seeing in your mind.

Think of it this way: If you go out and hit a thousand forehands and a thousand serves in tennis every day for the next year, you would get to a point where you'd really know how to serve a tennis ball and hit a forehand. You may not be Serena Williams or Roger Federer, but you would be very competent at hitting forehands and serving if you did it one thousand times a day for 365 straight days—that's a third of a million strokes. It would be quite a lot of physical practice that would pay off in the realm of form. Well, imagery, or visualization, is the equivalent of doing this but on the mental side. If you were to practice a thought a thousand times a day for a year, that image would become you and you would become that image. Visualization works because once you get the image, it gets stored away inside you exactly the same as a practice or behavior.

Let's say you want to lose 30 pounds, lower your resting heart rate, or quit smoking. You do nothing but have this image of yourself that you practice one thousand times a day: *I am not the poison. I am health. I am healing. I am not sickness. This is the picture I have of myself looking the way I want to look.* You draw that picture in your mind, and perhaps you even draw it on paper. You see this image everywhere, countless times a day, so you begin to internalize this message: *This is the way I look. This is the way I see myself. I'm not going to try to do anything differently. I just see myself as looking this way. I see myself as the picture of health.*

You don't think about quitting or losing, because those terms are negative. Understand that whenever you fight something, you violate the principle that holds the universe together. You are always weaker after you fight—always. Fighting anything is the surest way to set yourself up to fail. It's why the war on drugs doesn't work, for instance. A war by its very nature means that there must be winners and losers.

You can reshape your thinking so that you don't ever have to think in negatives again; instead, put things in terms of what you're *for* rather than what you're *against*. Now, rather than being against drugs and all the terrible things that they do, what if we could raise young people to be for something? After all, as a society, we're for an enlightened youth who are capable of getting themselves as high as they want to in their mind and in their consciousness. That seems like a much more effective message than fighting a war on drugs.

The more you fight, the more difficult you make it for yourself to understand that you're a human being and not a human doing. It's the *being* that you are. Let's say you want to stop eating so much chocolate. You see yourself as being someone who easily resists sweets, not telling yourself how difficult it will be or dwelling on how much you'll need to fight your cravings. Realistically, when you think about it, which is easier to do: eat chocolate or not eat chocolate? Think about what it takes to eat chocolate: You have to go to the store. You have to pay for it. You have to bring it home. You have to unwrap it. You have to put it in your mouth. You have to chew it. On the other hand, if you don't eat chocolate, all you have to do is not eat chocolate. That's all you have to do. So not eating chocolate is really a lot easier than eating chocolate, isn't it?

If you want to improve your tennis game, you don't tell yourself that this is a hard process. You see yourself the way you want to be, and you practice enough so that when you go out on the court and want to hit your forehand, you don't have to think about it anymore. I don't ever think about what I'm going to do with my racket. If I were thinking, *Where do I hold it? How do I hit the ball back? Am I going to step in?* I'd quickly lose three sets. I have practiced enough that I don't have to give my tennis game any thought—it has become instantaneous, automatic. Now I go out on the courts, somebody serves me a ball, and I hit a forehand. Somebody hits me a backhand, and I step into it and hit it back. I don't ever give it any thought. I learned how to do it through imagery, by seeing myself.

Do you know that every great golfer does the same thing? Jack Nicklaus has often talked about this. You see the shot going the way you want to see it. You see your swing the way you want to see it, and you practice the imagery over and over again. Before long, it's automatic. You see it, and then you just do it.

What if I were to ask you, "Are you a determined person?" You'd probably think of some obstacle you encountered and say, "Yeah, I gave it my best. I worked really hard. I sure did try, but it didn't work out. It wasn't my fate. I wasn't supposed to get it. I guess God doesn't want that for me."

Most of us believe we're persistent even if we try something only once. We say, "Yeah, I gave it my best." For how many days? "Oh, I only did it this morning, but I gave it a real shot." A single attempt is not a good test of determination, nor can it possibly prove whether visualization works. We have to try or practice repeatedly, and be willing to do *whatever it takes* to bring our image into form.

In fact, your willingness to do whatever it takes is the most important thing you can bring to the visualization process. If it takes moving, you move. If it takes leaving a relationship, then you do so. If it takes working 18 hours a day for 10 years, then you grind away, knowing that great things have no sense of time. You must be willing to act on what you imagine for yourself, understanding that what counts isn't being persistent but rather doing whatever it takes minute by minute, day in and day out. If you are willing to do that, you'll make what you're envisioning a reality. I have seen this play out in my own life, time and time again.

I've found that most of the people I've met who don't have what they want for themselves, or whose life isn't at the level they would like it to go, are not willing to do what it takes. They're willing to go only so far, and then they throw up their hands and say, "No, I can't do that. You mean you want me to leave here? I've been here all my life. You want me to go back to school and change careers? You want me to run eight miles? You want me to give up chocolate? You want me to keep doing that *every day?*"

Again, it's a question of how willing you are. If you are willing to do whatever it takes to turn your vision into reality, then you will be able to manifest that vision in myriad ways.

WHATEVER YOU WANT IS ALREADY HERE

There's an old story about a person who went to his guru and listed all the things that he wanted from life, such as wealth and happiness. The guru said, "I've got it for you." He gave the man a cup, which had nothing in it, and added, "You already have everything you need to be all those things. You already are that."

Once you get what the guru was saying, then you can appreciate it. You think about what you want for yourself, and you realize that what you're visualizing is already here. If you already know that whatever you have is what you created, then all you have to do is understand that whatever you want to create from this point on is entirely up to you. It's all done through something called "thought."

This is a crucial point: *Everything you could ever want is already here.* All the wealth and abundance that you could possibly ever want is already here. You've just got to tune in.

If you're willing and know that it's here, it can't miss you. That's the way the universe works.

Let's say you want to sell five million books. Well, what would that take? It would take five million people to buy one book, one million people to buy five books, or what have you, but the people who are going to buy your books are already here. In other words, the energy that is going to generate the wealth that you want is already here. You just haven't tuned in to it yet.

If you want wealth in your life, that wealth doesn't have to somehow materialize from another dimension. *Wealth is here.* Again, everything that you could possibly ever need or want for yourself is already here—you must know that and live that. If you believe that you need to have something else in order to be fully happy, then all you'll do is be in another place to not appreciate what you don't have. Like the man visiting his guru, you must know that you already are it all.

Of course, it's not like you can simply visualize yourself as wealthy, and then *poof*—you'll be wealthy. There are two things that go along with the endeavor. First, you visualize yourself as having wealth, enjoying abundance instead of scarcity. Then you see the abundance in your life and connect to that. You don't just tell yourself, *All right, now I've got that picture; now I'll sit around and wait for abundance to walk into my life.* We always have to *act on* whatever image we have.

So now you're beginning to act on a new image, which is one of abundance. You affirm: *I am entitled to have things improve in my life. There are no mistakes in the perfection that is this universe. I am part of the perfection of this whole universe. I am not separated out from humanity; I am a part of it all. Whatever God is, that is within me as well. I am Divine enough to ask, and I am important enough to receive.* These thoughts augment your image of abundance.

When you start acting on that positive, abundant, wealthy image you have, it won't be long until your actions take over. But again, what you're visualizing is here already. It's not going to arrive from Mars or someplace. If it wasn't here, you wouldn't be capable of visualizing it. How could you visualize what it would be like to be able to do something that is impossible for you to do? How could you visualize yourself being an entity that lives on Neptune when you hardly know anything about Neptune and have never been there? You wouldn't visualize yourself as some creature made out of gases or vapors. However, it is important to remember not to put limits on yourself when it comes to what you are capable of realizing here on planet Earth.

I read a very interesting study done with unemployed people who were asked to visualize themselves getting a job. One of the people had had a job that paid $25,000 a year. Another person's previous job had paid $50,000 a year. Another was an executive whose job had paid $250,000 a year. All three were told to practice this visualization technique: *See yourself with a job, see yourself working again, and then act on that visualization.* Each one of them did so, and as they saw themselves working again, that thought began to manifest itself and they began to act on it.

Three months later, all of the subjects were employed again. The first person, who'd had a $25,000 job, now had another $25,000 job. The $50,000-a-year person had a job paying that same salary. And the executive had a job paying $250,000. It wasn't because these individuals lacked special training or abilities that would keep them from having higher-paying jobs. They got the jobs that they saw themselves having; that's what they imagined for themselves.

A job isn't going to arrive from another planet; a job is already here. You just have to tune in to it now and connect to it. So if you imagine yourself working as a clerk and tell yourself, *That's all I'm capable of doing* and *I can't go beyond that,* then you look for and act on clerk kinds of images. Without the thought, you can't get the job. The job is a thought. Every day you get up and think, and then you get into your formation and go do your job.

The $50,000-a-year guy was a salesperson who saw himself continuing to make that salary, so that's what he went after. His vision was not one of abundance; it was of scarcity. It's like he told himself, *There's a limit on how much money I can make because of my history, because of my training, because of whatever it is that I've convinced myself of.* The executive went for another executive position and matched his previous salary as well. Everyone in the study essentially stayed at the same level they were before.

Examples like these preclude anybody from saying, "Yeah, all of this fancy higher-consciousness, spirituality, transformational kind of talk, it's very interesting and nice. If I've got time and all that, I'll get into it." Such people are missing the message that James Allen talked about: circumstances do not make a man; they reveal him.

WHERE ARE YOU PUTTING YOUR FOCUS?

Many of us find ourselves looking at our life backward, which is what the ego encourages us to do. It doesn't want us to face inward and contact the higher self, which encourages us to be present. We need to stop looking in a rearview mirror and turn toward the now, to see how our life can work in a new and authentically free way.

You can start by asking yourself this question: *What do I want to expand in my life?* If you want positive things to expand, for example, then keep thinking positive thoughts as much as possible. You'll act on that vision, and positivity will expand for you.

I once saw a wonderful story on TV about Mary Thomas, the mother of Isiah Thomas, the great basketball star of the Detroit Pistons. At one point she said, "I'm not poor. I've been broke, I've been without money, but I'm not poor. I've never been poor, and I never will be poor." This is the kind of consciousness that I'm talking about. If you focus on what you want to expand in your life instead of what you don't have, then what you focus on is going to expand.

When I was doing a radio show some years back, a man called in who was now a medical doctor. He had been one of 14 children growing up in a very poor part of Jamaica, but his grandmother always told him, "Your mind is more powerful than anything else." He was calling the show to validate some of the things I was saying on the air, because I was getting resistance from some of the people out there who were saying, "How can you say the kinds of things that you're saying to people who are in such poor circumstances? Don't you have any pity for them?" and so on.

I replied, "The whole focus of what I'm saying is that these are the people who need to hear what I've got to say the most. And that if you get yourself focused on what you want and never let your mind detract from that, then you'll act on that and eventually move out of those circumstances."

This fellow who called in shared how he had always wanted to be a doctor, and everybody laughed at the idea of this poverty-stricken boy, in this little village in Jamaica, ever becoming a doctor. "But my grandmother always said, 'Never get the idea out of your mind. Never, ever let that idea go. Just keep that thought there, no matter what.'"

He added, "I never did let it go; I always thought it. The more I thought it, the more I began to act on it. As I acted on it, I began to do two jobs instead of one, and then three jobs, and then I sent away for medical books, and I studied hard. I saved all my money, and I applied for scholarships."

This man proved that the ancestor to every action is a thought. All his actions came from one thought, which was, *I am going to be a doctor.* At the time of this radio show, he had a big practice in Washington, D.C., where he was a well-renowned heart surgeon. He had become a person of means, but he was also incredibly happy in his dream profession. And all of this had happened because he never got rid of the thought.

So when it comes to what you want to expand in your own life, keep focused on that thought, coupled with a strong image, and be willing to do whatever it takes to make it happen. When you do, you'll embody one of my favorite quotes of all time by Henry David Thoreau, which has been a guiding force my whole life: "If one advances confidently in the direction of his dreams, and endeavors to live the life which he has imagined, he will meet with a success unexpected in common hours."

CHAPTER 10

LEARN TO MEDITATE AND TRAIN YOUR MIND

It's not an accident that all the great spiritual masters have encouraged a kind of meditation practice of one kind or another. While most spiritually advanced people do it on a regular basis, I highly recommend meditation for everyone. You might have the false notion that meditation isn't for you; it's the kind of thing made up by some Far Eastern guru with a loincloth. If so, I want you to reframe that concept and know that it is a way to understand that there is another world available to us when we do it. I'm talking about the world of the mind.

When we go into that world, we discover many things about ourselves. For example, we become conscious of the thoughts that we have all the time and how much "disasterizing" we do—and how what we occupy our minds with is often so unnecessary, silly, foolish, and even destructive.

Recall that one of the keys to higher awareness is "shut down the inner dialogue." You want to be able to have an open, clear, and calm mind, not have a thousand thoughts rampaging through. Meditation will help you quiet your mind and hear your Divine wisdom.

THE IMPORTANCE OF TRAINING

Many of us seem to believe that whatever we think just sort of happens, and we can't help it. There's a thought, and it's simply there. It's what I call the pop-in theory of thinking: You're walking along and all of a sudden, *Wow. What was that? Well, now a thought popped in. I don't know how that happened. I was happy, but now I'm thinking really unhappy things. I guess I'll have to wait for them to pop out.* But remember that every thought you have is yours—it is your creation. You are the creator of your thoughts, which means that you are also the creator of your life. You can absolutely train your mind.

We spend so much of our energy training ourselves in all kinds of areas. We train ourselves or others how to work at myriad jobs, for instance. Or if we want to become good at golf or swimming or tennis or backgammon, we know we have to practice and train ourselves. Yet we ignore our mind, which is 99 percent of who we are. We completely ignore it, as if there's no training available for our minds. Of course there is, and we can all do it.

To that end, years ago, I taught at a university in Berlin for a semester, and I used a very effective technique for training the mind in memory retention. One the first day, I had a student introduce himself to me at the start of class. Then I had the second student introduce the person who had just introduced himself, then she introduced herself. Then each time I would repeat it. I had the third student introduce the two previous students, plus himself. We went along in this fashion for the whole class. By the time we got to the 70th student, that person had to introduce everybody in the class by name, and I then repeated each one of them. It was a very simple technique, a concentrated effort in making my mind remember 70 people's names in an hour and a half.

This was a class on how to identify neurotic behavior, and I wanted to teach the students that they could do things with their minds that they never dreamed they could. The name exercise was one simple yet effective way to show them what was possible for them: Two or three weeks later, the class would have 80 or 90 percent recall. By the end of the fourth or fifth week, everybody knew everybody else's name in the class, and they had all trained themselves.

I find it funny that when many people are introduced to somebody new, they immediately say, "What was your name again?" They can't remember one person's name in one minute. They think it's because they have a poor memory, but it's really because they haven't trained. Meditating is a perfect way to do that.

As you can see, learning to improve memory is very helpful. What's even more impactful, though, is keeping our minds free from worry, anxiety, or other stressful kinds of things. We can do this when we get focused and keep ourselves from creating those kinds of thoughts that are always impeding our consciousness. Miracles are available when we train our brains.

BE IN THE MOMENT

If you're the kind of person whose thoughts are filled with 10 different things you have to do, which is producing anxiety and stress throughout your body, then how can you possibly get a blank, quiet mind? You're thinking, *I've got to get to work. I have this report I need to do. I have to get my taxes done. I need to get some diapers on the way home. The kids need bananas. They've got dance lessons I've got to get them to.*

By simply going into your mind and looking around, you'll soon see how slimy it is and realize that occupying your mind with an endless catalog of activities is ridiculous and unnecessary. If you're the kind of person who takes care of things, they're going to get handled regardless of how much you worry. The question is: How do you use your present moments? Do you understand that anytime you are thinking anxious thoughts, you're denying the now? Instead of using up the present moment in a productive, serene, calm way, you are choosing to believe that you can't get through this day without being anxious.

The fact is everything is going to get taken care of. Your taxes are going to get done. You're not the kind of person who's simply going to opt out of doing your taxes. You're going to get the report done. You're going to get the diapers. You're going to get everything done; otherwise, you wouldn't be in the position that you're in. You would be doing something else.

So if you know that things are going to get done, then what would be the most efficient, effective, and peaceful way to do so? It's certainly not when you're in a hurry—that's when you're least effective. You'll feel anxious, which makes you feel more upset, and you'll forget something. You'll walk out the door and lock your keys inside.

Suppose you only have five minutes to take a shower. If you rush through, you'll find yourself sweating soon after you dry yourself off. You'll find you needn't have bothered with that shower because you're already dirty again. You can take the same five minutes and instead make it a peaceful experience. You can push all the other stuff out of your mind and just relax. Rather than rushing through the five minutes, you can experience the water. You can wash your body. You can dry it all off. When you finish, you won't be sweating, even though you had the same amount of time.

In the physical world, you understand that if you hurry and rush and are filled with a thousand different activities, you have decreased your efficiency. Well, the same thing is true in the mental world. If you are filling your mind with all the things you have to do, becoming consumed with your worries, your cluttered mind is not going to be very efficient or effective.

What if you're in the car at a moment like that? You can't simultaneously pick up the bananas and the diapers while typing out your report as you take care of the IRS—while you're driving. What you *can* do is take a deep breath and focus on the present. Put on some music and quiet your mind right there. Don't close your eyes, of course, but push all the negativity out. Tell yourself, *I'm going to enjoy this drive.*

One of my regular commutes is 17 miles. I love those 17 miles. There are a million things to see, and I can take note of them all. I can open the windows and feel the breeze. I can enjoy being present. Then when I get to where I'm going, if I've got to get the report done, I'll be fully prepared to do it. I won't be working on the report while thinking about my taxes, or getting the bananas, or whatever it may be. I'll be here now in the moment.

That's what meditation teaches you—how to be in the moment, quiet, peaceful, and joyful. When you train your mind, it isn't something you do for 15 minutes a day just to give you something to do for that 15 minutes. No, it carries over into everything that you do. The more peaceful you are, the more efficient you are. The more you're in a hurry, the more you're always trying to get someplace fast, the chances of having an accident are greater, the chances of getting there all ruffled are much greater, the chances of your heart rate going up or your stomach being upset are much greater. None of that is useful or worth it.

Meditation teaches you that you have the capacity to use your mind any way that you want to. You suddenly see that you don't have to join everybody else out there who is in a frenzy and all upset and worked up. It doesn't have to be that way for you.

KEEP ON PURPOSE

One day I was in a tennis match and not playing nearly at the level that I'm capable of. I had been meditating on a daily basis for quite a while at that point, and I decided right then to use tennis as a meditation. I was going to forget about winning or losing, forget about the score, and see if I could get out of my body. Or, I should say, get out of *the way* of my body, and allow it to do what it knows how to do, which is hit a tennis ball.

I started meditating right there on the court. I got really peaceful inside and began to put myself into that state where I get very light and don't notice distractions. It was absolutely incredible what I was able to accomplish in the next 45 minutes or so, when I had complete and total concentration on what I was doing. My body was incapable of making an error. I felt loose and easy, and it was so powerful. It was such a moving experience that I found myself doing this before I would speak, resulting in very happy, contented audiences.

Sometime after this tennis match, I had to have an uncomfortable conversation with someone. I chose to meditate my way through it, and it was an easy and harmonious experience. I realized that what I was saying to this person was both for their benefit as well as mine. It went well because I wasn't attached to any outcome at all. I was just allowing everything to flow.

136

Meditation has helped me gain peacefulness, serenity, and energy. One of the things I've discovered in the process is that my purpose is to love and to serve and to give, and I must evaluate every behavior, action, and thought I have in those terms: *Am I loving, serving, or giving?* I believe that all of us are actually here to give; we're not here to get. Meditation helps us tap into the Divine energy that shows us we are all here to serve each other and be in harmony.

In as little as 15 minutes a day, you too can get to the place where you're only letting harmony into your life. You won't even let anybody into your consciousness unless they come there with harmony. That's like a commitment you can make to yourself and others: *If you come with disharmony, discordance, anger, stress, or tension, you'll only get to my form. Unless you come with love, harmony, serenity, or peace, you won't get to who I really am. You won't get there because I'm beyond the need to have conflict and confrontation occupying my soul. I don't need that any longer; I'm past that. I no longer need to prove that I can deal with it or handle it. That's gone.*

This reminds me of an experience I had once while flying from Miami to San Francisco. The plane had just taxied out to the runway when the pilot announced that we wouldn't be able to take off. We'd have to go back to the gate because the stabilizer that takes care of the wing flaps or something wasn't registering as working properly. We were going to be delayed for a few hours while they fixed it.

My immediate attitude when something like that happens is, *I guess you're not supposed to get to San Francisco in five hours.* After all, when my ancestors wanted to get to San Francisco from Miami, if they left in September and got there in March, they considered that on time. It was a good trip if half the people were still alive. So if it's going to take me three more hours or whatever, that's okay. Plus, if the stabilizer isn't working on my aircraft—or in anything that stabilizes anything—I want to go back to the gate. I'm not interested in being angry about that. It's a part of surrendering and being at peace.

The flight attendant and I had been talking when the pilot made his announcement. She told me, "Oh, this is what I dread."

"What's the matter?"

"Look at all these people. Every one of them is going to say something nasty to me when they get off the plane. They're going to blame the airline, and they're going to blame me."

I said, "But you don't have to let that in."

"What are you talking about?"

"Well, you've got two packages that are protecting you from anybody coming to you with that disharmony," I told her. "You've got your uniform, which is one package. That's over the other package, which is your body. Both of those are covering, or protecting, who you really are, which is how you choose to think and process all of this.

"Every time someone says something negative to you, you can let that be a message only to your uniform, to your package. *That's not me,* you can remind yourself. *They're not talking to me. They can't get to me with that stuff. They can't have that. I don't let anybody reach who I really am unless they come with love or harmony.* As you're telling the person you're very sorry, you can tell yourself, *They didn't get to me. They're not reaching me with that.*"

Sure enough, she stood there and watched as scores of people got off, and many of them did say something nasty to her on the way out. Each time, she sort of smiled and gave them instructions on where to get help from the airline.

I stayed behind to see how it went for her. As the last person disembarked, she told me, "That was fantastic. This is the first time that we've ever had a circumstance like this where I didn't let it bother me."

I said, "You don't ever have to let stuff like that into your life. The more you keep it away from you, the more you allow yourself the right to have only what you want to enter your consciousness. I make this choice all the time. When I'm driving, for instance, and somebody gives me the finger, I don't take any of that inside. Instead, I think, *Oh, that's them, and that's how they're reacting to my form.* If somebody comes to me with love, serenity, peace, joy, ease, or the like, then they can have all of me. I will respond back with that. You let in whatever you want."

That's what a quiet mind does for you. Meditation allows you to select what you allow into who you really are without having to be beholden to every single person and action out there that doesn't fit in with the way you want it to be. Having a quiet mind, in a practical sense, is truly understanding that what I'm talking about here is not just for discussion—it's for application.

EVERYDAY BENEFITS OF MEDITATION

Please know that meditation doesn't require somebody teaching you exactly how to do it; in fact, that would defeat the purpose. I have meditated for a long time, but no one ever taught me how. I learned how to train my mind on my own, yet I've created miracles in that space for myself, as well as in the world that I came back to when I left the meditation.

I find it interesting that we create a light with our eyes closed in a dark room. We don't really need our eyes to create light, but we definitely need our minds. If you doubt that your mind is capable of creating illumination—or colors, smells, and sounds—remember that we do this all the time in our dreams, which is a state of pure thought. When you meditate, you want to get your mind to a similar place.

A self-hypnotic state is the first thing that you want to train yourself to get to. Here, you go into what is called an "alpha state." Like I said, you don't need to be taught exactly how to get here, but you may find inspiration in what I do: I use a 24-second shot clock, which is what they use at NBA games. It's got these little lights, starting at 24, then it counts down to 23, 22, and so on, to 1. If a thought of any kind enters my mind anytime between 24 and 1 (other than the picture of the number), I need to start over at 24. If I get to 16 and think, *Oh, I can't forget my dentist appointment tomorrow morning,* that's followed by the thought, *Back to 24 I go.*

Be patient with yourself as you practice meditating this way. You can use any sort of clock or timer that counts down, but you don't want to give yourself too much or too little time, so consider beginning with the number 24, like I do. It will take you a few days to get to 1 but keep at it. When you go from 24 to 1 without having an intervening thought, you will be in an alpha state.

You'll know that you've reached an alpha state when you raise your hands and your arms feel very light. Or your head will suddenly feel almost weightless, like you're starting to leave your form. Then after a few days or weeks, you'll be able to go into alpha without the 24-second clock. You'll be able to do it just through your breathing.

Once you feel comfortable getting into this alpha state, you can bring up topics to your higher self. You might ask questions that you have about your life, about struggles that you may be having with your children, about your relationships, about where you ought to be going, what kinds of decisions you're not sure about making, anything like that.

As you go into a meditative state, what happens is that you leave this world of form and enter into the formless, dimensionless world of thought. You then realize that you're the witness, watching yourself think and then react to the thought. You can ask yourself, *What's the solution to this? What can I do? Why is this a problem for me? Why am I creating this in my life? Why am I having such a difficult time with my partner? Why am I consistently clashing with this particular person on the job? What is it about me where I always set up myself to fail?* Answers begin to come, floating right into your consciousness from your higher self, from the Divine.

Now, how you apply this in your own day-to-day life becomes the very essence of awakening. You can meditate before a client meeting and see how you want it to work out. While you cannot control how other people are going to act or react, because that's for them, you are in control of yourself. You can certainly make an impact on how that other person is going to react to you with how at peace you are with yourself and how unattached you are to the outcome. You're focusing on *How I can serve this other person?* rather than *What is going to come to me?* You can do this in all of your relationships: look for the beauty and joy in your own mind, and see how you want those relationships to be.

When I first got into a regular meditation practice, I would feel so blissful toward everybody I saw I could hardly stand myself. I would just look at them and think, *Ah, aren't they terrific?* I had this connectedness with everyone I came face-to-face with, from my family members to complete strangers. Blaise Pascal once said that "All of humanity's problems stem from man's inability to sit quietly in a room alone," and that makes sense to me. I could never imagine wanting to hurt anybody after coming out of that state.

When talking about meditation, I also like to use the example of having two selves: one self is a thought and the other self is in form. If you say to yourself, *You jerk, you shouldn't have done that*, you've got two people there. You've got the person who is doing the name-calling—that is, the thought who is saying "you jerk"—and then you've got the jerk, who is the body that has to react to what kind of thoughts you have. So if you call yourself a jerk, you have a thought of jerk and you have the jerk who has to react. Meditation can help you to bring those two selves into harmony so that self one, the thought, and self two, the body, are in unity. You are only calling yourself what you want yourself to be, and you are only seeing what it is that you want in your mind for your body to do.

You can start to apply this by closing your eyes and getting into a very quiet space. In fact, all you have to do if you don't have time to meditate is take the last hour before you go to sleep and use it in this way, because it will give you a strong sense of total rest and relaxation, like you've never experienced before. An hour of meditation will give you eight hours of deep, restorative sleep. It's that powerful.

It's said that this practice can even alter our own chemistry. You can use meditation to reach an ecstatic, beautiful, exquisite high state that people so desperately look for in chemicals. I think it would be especially beneficial to teach young people about the power of their mind, so that they wouldn't be tempted to chase counterfeit freedom. Personally, meditation has always filled me with the most wonderful sense of peace and harmony. It's a magnificent feeling, like you really are in touch with God.

THE LAWNMOWER MANTRA

There's a nice story of a man who was bothered by a car honking for his neighbors next door. He said to his wife, "If I had magical powers, I would be able to give that car four flat tires every time he comes here. Or I'd be able to put a silencer on that horn and wouldn't even be able to hear it. That's what I would do if I had magical powers." She replied,

"No. If you had magical powers, you wouldn't be disturbed by that horn at all."

Quieting your mind means that you're no longer susceptible to all of the external influences that are around you. For an example of this, you can watch the US Open Tennis Championships, which are played in New York, right near LaGuardia Airport. I'm always amazed when I see how the players are able to play with the distraction and noise of jets flying overhead. Yet when I've been really involved in a tennis match myself, I've had jackhammers going next to me and not noticed them. My opponent could be going crazy from the noise, but all my concentration is on the ball. The people who are really good at a game, or any activity that requires concentration, know how to do that.

This makes me think of something that happened when I was on vacation in Hawaii with my family some years ago. For seven days in a row, I got up at 5:30 every single morning and went out to meditate in a grassy area next to our hotel.

One day I was sitting on my mat, and I was in a blissful state. I felt a Divine energy going up and down my spine, and it felt so good. All of a sudden, I heard this noise. *Vrrm vrrm. Vrrm vrrm vrrm vrrm vrrm vrrm vrrm.* I looked up, and there was a mean-looking guy with a cigarette in his mouth and tattoos covering his arms. I realized that even though it was very early in the morning, he was going to cut the grass. My first thought was, *Oh, no.* I stood up, gathered my mat, and started to leave. Then all of a sudden, my intuition came to me and said, "Go back. Go back and use this. This is a metaphysical experience." It's not that I was hearing voices; this was an internal thing.

I thought, *Huh?* But I put the mat back down, and within about two minutes I went right back into my meditative state. My intuition said, "Use the lawnmower for a mantra."

So every time I heard, *Vrrm vrrm vrrm vrrm*, I'd think to myself, *Oh yes*. I got back into that blissful state.

The guy cutting the grass came by my mat, and the sound was incredibly loud. I thought, *God, I'm here and I'm listening, but why would You send this person to me at six in the morning? I see, this is a test.*

After about 10 minutes, he finally finished, and I was happy he was done. I was getting back into that very peaceful place when I heard the loudest noise I have ever heard in my life. My friend was back, and he had an edger this time. As God is my witness, this guy decided to edge my mat. *Brrrrrrrrrrrrrrr.*

I thought, *Okay, God. I'm going to use the edger for a mantra. I'm staying here. I've got to turn this into something.* He went right by my mat, *Brrrrrrrrrrrrr.* I stayed with it. I didn't let the distraction get to me. It was about half an hour of this, but the louder the edger got, the easier it got for me.

He finished his yard work, and I finished meditating. I'll bet he thought, *Boy, this guy is in some kind of trance, or he's dead. One or the other.* It really felt as if I had come out of a trance. When you end such a meditation, it's like you can fly. You can do anything, and all you have is love, all you have is harmony, all you have is peace for yourself and for the world. Nobody and nothing can get to you, no matter what.

As I walked toward this guy, I could see he was very tense. Now keep in mind that I was about a foot taller than him. He probably thought, *This is what I'm here for. This guy's going to fight me.* I reached into my pocket, where I found about eight dollars, and gave them to him. I said, "Thank you so much for being here. I really needed you today." He looked at me like, *I don't know what's going on here,* but I smiled and walked away.

It was the greatest evidence I've ever experienced to prove that when life hands you lemons, you can make lemonade. I was taught that day that everything that comes to you, you have the power in your mind to turn it into whatever you want. We all get lawnmowers coming into our lives every day. What we do with them and how we handle them, well, that is the way to our personal transformation.

CHAPTER 11

LIVE IN THE LIGHT

Ram Dass tells one of my favorite stories of all time. It's about his guru, with whom he lived and worked for years in India, a man he considered to be the most spiritually advanced person he'd ever met in his life.

At that time Ram Dass was doing some experimenting with Timothy Leary and the like, so he had three capsules of LSD with him. "That would be enough," he said, "to put a horse into a tranquilized state for several days." He had planned to use this LSD for a number of months, just one or two micrograms at a time.

His guru said to him, "You have funny medicine . . . let me see it." Ram Dass showed him the capsules but warned, "You don't want to take all three of these. You should only take a few micrograms from one of the capsules, and that will give you the desired effect."

His guru took all three capsules, put them in his mouth, and swallowed. He went under his blanket, and then came out and did all these funny things. Then he smiled and said, "Do you have any more? It doesn't seem to be working."

Ram Dass realized that the drugs had no effect on his guru at all. This was his conclusion, which is one of the greatest lines I've ever heard on this subject: "If you're already in Detroit, you don't have to take a bus to get there." In other words, when someone is already in the spiritual world, they don't need anything to get them there.

Learning how to "get to Detroit" for us means achieving what we've been talking about in this book. It's when we are comfortably in the place that is powerfully ours. It's when we understand that thought originates with us, which means that life is our own creation. We know that our form will simply pass along, but we can't kill thought, so who we really are can never die.

When you are truly awake, with heightened spiritual awareness, you know that if you're always looking for something, it will always elude you. That's true of anything in life. Take success: Making a lot of money is not what makes a person successful. Rather, a successful person brings success to everything that they do, and money is most likely only one of the benefits that they get as a result.

Enlightenment is the same thing. Enlightenment is something that you bring to all of your interactions, all of your thought processes, all of your life experiences. It's really an attitude or an approach to life. That attitude or approach is literally one of "living in the light," and that means you're moving toward yourself. You're not ever moving away from yourself, and you see the perfection in yourself and who you are. You don't question the universe. You see everything and everyone in it as exactly where they're supposed to be. You have an absence of judgment and negativity. You're balanced as a human being.

Enlightenment is a state of mind in which, once you have it, once you accept yourself and your perfection, then there's no more trying. You are already in Detroit.

IT ALL WORKS PERFECTLY

Think about this: If you take a bite of food and start to chew, you've got to do a lot of things with that food in order to make it apply to you. Let's say you just had a bite of salad, and now you've got lettuce and tomato in your mouth. Well, you've got to get some saliva into your mouth as well to help you with that. You're not trying to salivate; your body knows exactly what it's supposed to do. When you swallow, you don't have to monitor the peristaltic reactions in your throat and esophagus to make sure that food goes down instead of up. It never goes up into your nose—well, maybe once in a while, if you're doing something really silly. But you don't eat your food and say, "Oh, wait a minute, I put it into my nose. It's not supposed to go there." It goes where it's supposed to, and then it breaks down.

You don't have tomatoes and a great big piece of lettuce floating around through your body, saying, "Where are we supposed to go?" You chew them up, and different kinds of enzymes attack the pieces of food. It all goes exactly where it's supposed to, through the digestive system and then to all different parts of your body—your pancreas needs a little lettuce today, perhaps. Without some component of the tomatoes, maybe your toes are going to fall off. Every place in your body gets the proper nutrients without your having to do anything.

You're not going around saying, "Oh my, I've got to get all this done. I've got so much to do with this digestion. I've got to make sure that my pancreas and duodenum work. Ugh, how do I turn this lettuce into waste? How am I going to get that out?" You're not busy doing any of that. It all works in harmony and perfection. Your heart is beating, and it does so thousands of times every single day.

You don't need to tell your heart to pump blood for it to do so perfectly. You don't have to do any of it, yet you are controlling it all.

Enlightenment is like that: You get in harmony, and you start functioning optimally. Who you are as a human being just happens. It all works. You don't have to go around thinking every minute, *Is this an enlightened response? Am I using higher consciousness here? I don't know if I'm being spiritual enough. Do I need to adjust?* You don't have to do that any more than you have to beat your heart or operate your digestive system. It all works perfectly when you're in harmony. If you're not, then it's as if you were trying to direct the tomato and lettuce to the right places. You would get so mixed up and puzzled by it.

If you tried to beat your own heart, you couldn't. You naturally let it work. This is the same way you must see yourself within the universe—allow yourself to work perfectly. The way you do so is to focus on yourself while also having respect and love for everyone. These universal laws that we're talking about here are the very same ones that are in place for your digestion or your cardiopulmonary system. The necessary enzymes are released instantaneously, and it all happens in a perfect way. There are certain rules and laws that apply to everything we do, from how we relate to each other to how our bodies function.

Sometimes after hearing me speak or reading my books, people will come up to me and say, "I'm a seeker too." They assume that I'm this way because I talk about the higher truths, principles, and laws that are universal yet elude so many people. This kind of amuses me, so I'll respond, "I'm not a seeker. I'm not looking for anything. I'm evolving, going through the dream, and enjoying it all. I am bringing this mind-set to everything that I do."

When you're in harmony with these transcendent laws, you are in enlightenment. You're not seeking it. You don't have to understand it, and you don't have to agree with it. You simply know that it is. In fact, enlightenment is nothing more than the quiet acceptance of what is.

Your desire to make things better is also part of what is, so you learn to go with that. When you are focused on making things better—helping, serving, extending love—and are able to send that out into the world, you are now a part of the spiritually aware, awakened consciousness.

THE THREE STAGES OF ENLIGHTENMENT

I've found that there are three specific stages of enlightenment. The first stage is learning by hindsight. As an example, I think about this woman who told me: "Ten years ago, my husband came home from work, said, 'I'm leaving you,' and walked out. I was devastated. For years, I couldn't get over it. But now I can look back on his leaving me as the most important turning point in my life. I see the blessing in it." After years of suffering, she was able to come to the realization that his leaving her was a blessing, not a tragedy. In other words, this stage of enlightenment is reached through a lot of understanding of the past. You do not immediately embody the present-based knowledge that there's an opportunity in every obstacle.

In the next stage, you do: you understand in your heart that everything that comes your way is a blessing. You see that this is more than just a hokey phrase used in self-help. In fact, what I've been talking about in this book is not self-help but *self-realization*, which is way beyond self-help.

When you begin to realize yourself—when you discover your magnificent potential—you see that everything that's coming at you has an opportunity in it, even though it may look like an obstacle. You think, *I wonder why I created this. I wonder what lesson is in this for me.* You may still have the suffering, but it's minimal and doesn't last. Rather than 10 years, for example, you might move through a challenging situation in 10 weeks, 10 days, 10 minutes maybe.

Suffering is always played out in form because it comes from your thoughts. Because you know that what you think about expands, you learn not to focus on the negative. Let's say you're going through a divorce, a tough time financially, an illness, or a death in the family, whatever it is. Now you're looking at it as, *I can get something out of this. I can grow from this. I can transcend and go past it.* Your mind is focused on that instead of on, *Why is this happening to me? Someday I'll know why, but I don't know why today. It's so terrible that I'm going to be depressed for six more years.* You don't go there anymore. Thinking like this belongs back there in another time in your life. You're solidly in the second stage.

People ask, "If that's the second stage, what else is there?" Well, the third stage of enlightenment happens when you are able to get out in front of things. You see them coming and play them all out in thought, and then you decide which of these is going to be brought into form.

For example, let's say you're in a relationship and your partner says something upsetting to you. You know that if you respond in a certain way, then she's going to respond in kind. Then you're going to say this, and she's going to say that—you can play that all out in thought, and you're out in front of it already. You can even see how this could devolve into an absolute blowout, with both of you really upset for two or three days, maybe not talking, maybe storming out, or doing any number of things that people do to avoid being intimate.

Again, you play that all out and know you don't have to make it happen. You don't have to make her wrong, which is a great step. You don't have to make you right, an even higher step. There's no right or wrong here. You play everything out, and as you do, you decide that you don't have to bring this altercation into form. You got out in front of it; it's gone. It's all been played out in your mind. You use your mind to *not* bring into form, into your life, into action that which you know is not beneficial for either one of you.

In relationships, this means letting go of your need to be right and instead celebrating the differences in the other person, and agreeing to disagree about them for the rest of your life if necessary. I tell people that this is a wonderful stage to get to, because once you and your partner are both there, you can still express your perspective. You don't have to be a certain age to get to this point—you can learn it at any time in your life.

As you move across the levels of enlightenment, you go from being an actor in the first stage, being directed by events, circumstances, and other people, to being the director yourself in the second stage. Then in the third stage, you become the producer too. You are now the actor, the director, *and* the producer of your entire life, and you're doing it all with your mind. If it's a career move that you once would have agonized over, you can see how it's going to go. If you're living in Atlanta but need to go to Houston, you can see yourself selling your home and driving to Texas to start this new job or enterprise.

When you play all this out, you can actually see how everything is going to work, because what you think about expands. Then you can decide. Your decision isn't based upon, *My boss is going to do this to me, and the world is going to do this, and if these things don't work out* . . . It's based upon your projecting in your mind how you want things to be. If the picture doesn't come out exactly the way you want it to be, then you're out in front of it already, and you don't go to Houston after all. Or perhaps you do choose to move because you see it as an exciting, wonderful adventure and a time to do something new. And you can do these steps with anything that you perceive to be coming at you but is really what you're creating through all the choices that you're making.

You can use your mind in exciting ways, as I said. On the job, you can see how, if you react in a certain way toward your boss or co-worker, you know that *If I say or do this, that that's going to set them off. I don't have to go there anymore. Instead of behaving like A, B, C, or D, I've already done it all in my mind, and I've seen the result. I don't want to go there. I don't want my form to have to follow that any-more, so I'm in front of it.* It's like you're producing your life through your mind.

WIN-WIN SOLUTIONS

The totally awake and aware person has almost moved beyond success. Success in Western society tends to mean accumulation or winning rather than achievement. It almost always means you have to outperform or get more than the other guy. This is very much a part of our culture, and there's nothing wrong with it. But now you understand that success, achievement, and performance all have built into them the notion that somebody else has to lose in order for you to win. When you are enlightened, you learn to approach conflict from a win-win position. While this has become a popular slogan and philosophy in business, it can also be used in any type of interpersonal situation.

I think very strongly that when you are in a romantic relationship, you fall in love with the things in another person that you don't have in yourself. After all, to fall in love with somebody who has everything exactly the same as you is to have a redundant relationship. You've already got that; what do you need more of it for?

Yet people will say, "Oh, we have so much in common. He says this, and I say the same thing; he likes to do this, and I like to do it too. He's an athlete, and I like athletes." They think it's such a wonderful thing that they have all these things in common. I always think, *Uh-oh, this one's doomed. We've got some real problems here.* But when someone says, "Ah, she's the exact opposite of me," I think that's almost always where the most intensity is found. When this couple looks at each other, they realize, *They are many things that I am not and can't be, and I like that. I like having that around me. I need that passion around me. I need that person who talks a lot around me, because I'm very quiet.* This is what endears them to each other.

What often happens, though, is that as time passes in a relationship, you forget that the differences are what give it spice. Then you turn those differences, which are the very thing that attracted you to the person in the first place, into areas of conflict or confrontation. You begin to try to alter the person you love. This does not make them think that you love them, but rather that you want them to be different. You have to remember to go back to what you fell in love with.

All relationships are about an opposite. You don't need a mirror of yourself—you've already got that. Even with your children, the things that usually endear you the most to them are the things they do that are not like you. Those are often the things you respect the most. You admire, for example, your child who will stand up for what she thinks is right and take the slings and arrows that go along with such fearlessness. Of course you don't want her to be contrary and disobedient, but there's a part of you that says, "You know, I never had the courage to do that myself. I don't want her to ever not do that." When you admire such qualities, you can learn from them, and they become your teachers.

You can make something very positive and beautiful out of those differences. When you make conflict something to honor, to dance with, to celebrate, you become instantly focused on solutions. Most often, the solution to the differences in any relationship lies in respecting, honoring, and celebrating the very things that are different in the other person. Again, you bring a win-win attitude to it.

So when conflict crops up at work, you have to take the same approach. Resist the urge to be problem-oriented— that is, *I'm going to make this person wrong, and I'm going to make myself right*—or turn it into a contest. You do not need to feel threatened by the differences in other people. You see that others are on a different part of the path than you are. Some people are very efficient at getting things done, while others are slower. Instead of making them wrong, you can refrain from being ego-involved in this at all.

I think this one of the hardest things for us in the try-to-get-ahead-of-the-other-guy, competitive-oriented West to grasp. Yet we must try to get to the point where the differences in other people are to be respected and honored, accepted for what they are rather than treated as contests. Bringing in a spiritual, right-brained, intuitive kind of approach isn't going to make you wimpy, weak, or less profitable; in fact, it will bring you peace and harmony. It will give you a sense of knowing what you're about and why you're here, and that lack of the need to be right or to win or to put somebody else down frees you up to do better.

I have moved much more in this direction in my own life. I don't need to make a contest out of every difference I have with others; instead, I recognize those variations and look toward solutions. I dance with, even enjoy, the discord rather than treat it as something that shouldn't be there.

Since I've given up some of my attachments to having to be right and embarked upon a path of sending out love and peace and harmony and contentment, I've never had more "success" come into my life. My books and audio programs are very popular. The demand for my lectures has increased, and people are inviting me to do things that never even came to me before, such as create my own television shows and write plays. Success as viewed in an external fashion, as an achievement, has certainly gone up for me. Yet I'm talking about going beyond all of that.

Again, the great irony is that when we get focused on following our bliss and being in the service of others, all those things that we seek so desperately—the success, the achievement, the performance—seem to arrive in our lives in great amounts. But as long as we find ourselves pushing for, demanding, chasing after, and striving for them, they will never arrive. The only vehicle that's available to take us from striving to arriving is detachment and acceptance.

A NEW KIND OF APPROACH

When you are enlightened, you no longer see yourself as separated from higher consciousness. Instead, you see it as what you are. Then you start having dramatic new changes in your life.

That old focus on accumulation and having to get things done is no longer there, so you become much more peaceful. Then after a while you realize that *Everything that I'm doing is all right. Even when I mess up, even when the deal doesn't go through, there's something to learn. There's an opportunity in that obstacle or in that failure.* You get this incredible peace with all the things that you're doing.

You see that this world of form is all an illusion and that you are destroying yourself with things that aren't even real. Why should you concern yourself with whether this person likes you or doesn't, whether you get that money or not, and all that? You can't do anything with that anyway. You tell yourself, *I'm going to stop messing myself up. I won't even think like that any longer.* Before long, instead of being full of anger and disharmony, you become full of acceptance. You have a new kind of approach to all that you're doing in your life, and the only thing that matters is love.

Deep inside you—in that special place where you know that you are thought and thought is you, and you are a higher consciousness—you feel more productive and less consumed with what other people are thinking. You find yourself moving away from all the stuff that used to be such an important part of your life, trying to get this one to like you and trying to please that one, or being in an overbearing or controlling relationship. You leave that all behind. You avoid confrontation and conflict because that isn't you any longer. You're much more peaceful with everything.

After a while, you look for the beauty in what others do, and you see it in everybody. Somebody will cut you off on the freeway, somebody will yell at you, somebody will be obnoxious toward you, somebody will not pay their debt toward you—any number of things that at one time would have driven you absolutely insane—and you understand, *That's where they are on the path.* You know that everything that happens to you and everybody you run into in your life are gifts. They teach you something about yourself. You think, *All those people are just tests for me to see whether I can, in fact, send them something positive and useful and not let them get to me.*

The minute a negative person starts getting to you, what you've really done is given up control of your life to them.

You've communicated that their opinions of you are more important than your own are. If you see that person for where they are on the path, recognizing that the way they behave has nothing to do with you, then you're not going to make yourself miserable because they choose to act toward you in that way. Before long, you can turn those kinds of people around.

Take three people looking at a given situation: one of them sees the anger, another one sees the hostility, and another one sees the love behind it all. The person who sees the love behind the encounter, wherever it may be, has a much better chance of not only getting what they want but also helping to turn others around. For example, think of an airport, where there are a lot of people fighting over how they're going to get seated on a plane. I have found myself in a similar situation to this many times. There will be several people acting aggressively toward a clerk who is trying to do her best and be as polite as she can. But the person who is antagonistic can only see the antagonism in another person.

I'll be admiring how well the attendant is handling all of the people giving her a hard time. I recognize what a kind person she is and how she's trying to do her absolute best. When it's my turn to get up there, I'll say, "Wow, you're really having to struggle. You sure have to put up with a lot when you do a job like this, but you handle it so well and don't lose your cool." You know what? She will often go out of her way for me. I might get moved up to first class, get the very seat that I want, or simply be rewarded with a genuine smile.

When you're looking for the good, you can make almost any situation turn around for you. After a while, this becomes a habit, and you don't even see the negative because you don't have that in you. On freeways, you wave to people and thank them for letting you in. You expect that somebody will let you in, but even if they don't, you don't internalize that action. You don't rant, "These people, who do they think they are?" You let it all go. You let them go right by, and you look to the next person. Before long, someone will put their hand out and let you in. You smile and say thank you, and you get what you want for yourself without having to be attached or hang on to all the negativity that most people see. You are living in the light.

Swami Mukundananda had a wonderful line. He said, "Enlightenment is your ego's greatest disappointment." This is certainly the truth, as it is the language of the higher self, all the way. It is a sign that you are totally awake and aware, in touch with the Divine nature of who you really are. You no longer need to try; you are. You have arrived.

CHAPTER 12

ENJOY HEAVEN ON EARTH

As we finish this book's journey, let's return to the course we charted at the beginning. If you were able to suspend your disbelief and keep an open mind, you may feel a kind of expansiveness as you pushed past the limits you previously felt comfortable with. Things that were once unavailable to you, based on the consciousness you had when you first started reading this book, probably feel within your grasp now. As we wrap things up now, I'd like to illuminate some of the benefits you can expect once you are in tune with the higher part of yourself, telling the ego to take a back seat.

BLESSINGS OF THE HIGHER SELF

When you are totally awake, aware, and enlightened, you receive some of the most powerful blessings of the universe. These come via your higher self, which is the Divine speaking through you.

THE POWER OF AWAKENING

— **You experience a drastic reduction in the amount of stress you have.** This is one of the most important things that happen. You realize that being strongly self-centered is actually what brings on stress. The more stress you have, the more the ego is controlling you. When you're not insisting on having what you want, in this particular way, in this particular timeline—all the while urging others to jump through hoops in order for you to have it—you are much more peaceful.

Anyone with stress is subject to rigid likes and dislikes. Such strict adherence means an absence of freedom for you, which can in turn manifest as countless stress-related illnesses. Why should any part of your life be at the mercy of the ego? It's like turning control over to something outside of yourself, and of course the moment you do that you're no longer free.

If you don't have the inflexible need to have things go the way you want them to—if you're able to go within and allow the peaceful, loving, centered part of yourself to take over—you find that those strong likes and dislikes turn into mild preferences. After a while they aren't even preferences anymore, because you're not attached to how things turn out. Not being attached to the outcome is really your higher self at work.

When you are calm, patient, and compassionate, you respond to life with that very calmness, patience, and compassion. This gives you an enormous benefit, such as reducing the physiological reactions that come from being an angry, irritated, easily annoyed individual. You find yourself less at the mercy of the ego, which really likes to keep you out of balance and off center. It wants to keep you in a state of conflict because when you have difficulty and struggle, then you won't turn to your higher self, which is what the ego always fears the most.

Of course life has its storms, but you are able to keep calm right in the middle of any turbulence. This isn't even something you have to do deliberately: As you become more serene and reliant on your higher self, you'll naturally find yourself less and less irritated. Your blood pressure won't be affected by an insult, your heart isn't going to have to race when you're contradicted, and all the vital parts of your body are going to function optimally. What a powerful idea that is for you—every single aspect of your whole body working not because you are healthier, but because you're no longer at the mercy of all of these external stimuli that are controlling you. You have achieved *authentic freedom.*

— **You have an absence of resentment.** You realize that the ego tries mightily to keep you focused on yourself and all the things that are seemingly very important to you. When you let go of that and allow the Divine within you to rule, when you embrace higher awareness, what happens is that resentment seems to go out the window.

A resentful person is someone who finds occasions for offense almost all the time, tending to see it just about everywhere they go. In this way, driving on the freeway can be an occasion for resentment. Family members not doing things how they should is another occasion for resentment. The cat scratching on the furniture instead of on the post, or the refrigerator not having any beer in it at the moment, can be occasions for resentment. Reading the news and finding out that one political party said this, and another one said that—there's another occasion for resentment. On and on it goes, until pretty soon they become someone who's looking for resentment in virtually everything they see, which just means that the control of their life isn't theirs.

Authentic freedom comes when you can go through your days and see such things not as occasions for resentment, but as the way they are. As for those things that you'd like to see changed, you can work at changing them without being self-absorbed. The more you meditate, the more peaceful you get, and the more you get to know the God force that is within all of us. You discover that the universe is on purpose, and all the things that are happening are part of God's plan, even though you don't understand them. I think one of the greatest insights you can have is that the Divine plan works and yours doesn't. If it did, you wouldn't be having any of these kinds of resentments or be so self-absorbed.

— **You become more productive and have more energy.** The less you are attached to outcome and self-absorption, the more energy you have left over for what you're here for in the first place. The ego says, "You must be concerned with everything." The higher self says, "If you surrender, serve, go with the flow, have an overriding spiritual objective, and know that you are here for a purpose, there will not be time for what offends you."

As you go through the process of moving from your ego to the higher part of yourself, you open up an energetic gateway. You can then try a very powerful thing called "recapitulation," which is a whole process that I truly believe in. I've read some works by people who have done it, and they said that every experience you've ever had in your life is there. The process helps you remove the negative energy from your life, and when you do, you open up a space for new, positive energy. It's as if removing something from this place inside of you opens up an opportunity for God to come in.

I did this recapitulation process myself through meditation. I went back to my fourth-grade class and saw Fred there next to me. In front of Fred was Janice, and then there was Earlene, and then Mrs. Engel was sitting at the head of the class. I said, "My God, I was able to get the entire fourth-grade class! They are all there."

This was the year my mother had taken my brothers and me out of the orphanage. I found that I could move the energy of that time—all this stuff that I had stored, the anguish I was feeling, the anticipation that things were going to get better but then they didn't. My mother remarried somebody who was just like my father—she hadn't learned her lessons yet, so she went through another cycle with another abusive, alcoholic man until she got it. Through recapitulation, I was able to let all that energy go.

You can go back and send out of your own life any negative energy that has accumulated, which will also help to open yourself up. Returning to what we learned earlier in the book, cultivating the witness doesn't only mean that you watch yourself; it's a process of detaching yourself from your problems and understanding that you are not whatever troubles you. You get to a point where you can understand that nothing in your life is going or has ever gone wrong; everything is and always has been the way it's supposed to be.

When you allow the higher part of yourself to focus on what's right with the world instead of what's wrong, you become more productive. Releasing negativity from your life, and not allowing the ego or your self-absorption to get in the way, helps you feel more powerful, in control, and at peace. I know recapitulation changed my entire outlook, and I had much more energy after experiencing that.

— **You discover what your deep, driving desire is.** Personally, it seems that the reason I showed up on this planet has something to do with teaching self-reliance. I haven't been able to escape it at any time in my life. When I was a little boy living in the orphanage and various foster homes and the new children would come in, the folks in charge would ask, "Where's Wayne?" Some little girl would be crying, and they'd say, "Wayne, why don't you come talk to her." I'd take my new friend by the hand and say, "It's a great place, and you're going to have such a good time. There are no parents here or anyone telling you what to do all the time. It's fantastic." This was when I was six or seven years of age, and I've been doing it ever since.

When I was in high school, I wrote essays and even novels about these kinds of issues of self-reliance. When I was in the military, I gave courses on epistemology and self-directedness on my own time. I'd get 30 guys coming to my "classes," and we'd discuss these kinds of things. I also helped people who were having to deal with the system there, all the bureaucracy and regimented rules. Then I got out and went to college, and when I started teaching, I would have after-school seminars about the subjects that we've talked about in this book. I've been living this stuff for as long as I can remember. This deeper, more purposeful part of my life seems to be what I showed up on earth for.

When you get tuned in to what your purpose is and that becomes your primary motivator, you have an overriding spiritual objective. You know that all the petty things you encounter on a daily basis are simply minor distractions from your deep desire. You don't need anyone's approval, nor will you feel the need to dominate others. As you tame your ego and leave behind your self-importance, you become focused on what you're here for. Your energy is placed only on that, nothing more, and anything that anybody else says that's in opposition to that will be seen as just where they are on the path. You won't disagree or feel annoyed with them; as a matter of fact, you won't even notice it because your energy will be concentrated solely on what you're here for.

— **You won't ever be lonely.** The ego promotes loneliness because the more alone you feel, the more you try to fill the void with external pursuits. When you don't feel any void within you, it's easy to love whom you're alone with, which is your higher self. Loneliness is impossible for you.

You also know that we're all one and we're all connected. There's a Divine energy that flows through all of us, so there's no possibility of ever experiencing alienation. You now have the ability to love much more powerfully, which reduces the possibility of your living with broken relationships. You live according to your higher self, which promotes peace, fulfillment, integrity, and joy. The very energy that you are, the force that holds every cell together, the glue that holds the universe together, is something that we call love. This glue is who you are. Once you discover and experience that, then you see only through the eyes of love and acceptance.

The ego wants you to live with fear, which is the opposite of love. It urges you to feel that you're incomplete or there's something wrong with you, which comes from that fear. But you know that you don't have to make anyone wrong, and you don't have to make yourself right, because you're not separate from them. You see the fullness of God in them, and you allow and love that Divine part of them.

I remember my friend Deepak Chopra once telling me a story about a famous Indian saint who was being escorted into some very fancy place. Right as he was about to step onto the red carpet that had been prepared for him, a beggar appeared. One of the people who was with the saint said, "Get out of the way! Can't you see that we have a master coming through?" The beggar looked up and asked, "Who is it that you're asking to get out of his way? Is it this body, or is it the god that is within me?" And the saint bent over, kissed the man, and said, "You don't have to move aside; we are both one."

That kind of awareness becomes something you consistently practice, for it's a way to take your relationships and imbue them with harmony. Since you know that we're all connected, there is an absence of discord.

— **You become a more powerful human being.** You are more powerful than you've ever even considered before, but not in the sense that most people think of it. As Gandhi once said, "Strength does not come from physical capacity. It comes from an indomitable will." You will create that strength of your indomitable will, which really means that you're going to stop associating who you are with your form. Many people identify themselves with who they are based upon their bodies; they say that if their bodies are not working the way they think they should, then that's an excuse to become impatient, less loving and caring, and so on.

If your power comes from your physical prowess, then when your physical prowess leaves, that means you're no longer a powerful human being. Of course you know that your power doesn't come from that; it won't dissipate when your form dissipates. You know not to give in to every single pleasure or selfish desire that comes along; you only ever treat your body in a healthy way. You have changed the identification of yourself away from your embodiment to your higher self, and you are free.

— **You discover the ultimate security.** It's as if someone once told you that trees were glued to the ground, and you believed it. Then an expert came along and told you that was false; there are roots under trees. The expert helped you dig a bit beneath the soil, and sure enough you saw the truth.

This whole process of finding security is like discovering that you have roots beneath the surface too. You have unearthed parts of yourself that you never knew were there, and you enjoy a security that you never experienced before when you identified so closely with your form.

— **You know that any problem you have is to be solved in the mind.** That's a very powerful insight, and it's a freeing one as well. When you have a struggle or conflict, when you are provoked or contradicted and it manifests itself physically, you know it's really a problem to be solved in thought. You know that what your body is reacting to is nothing more than how you are choosing to process something. Recognizing that it's your own reaction causing you stress, anxiety, tension, fear, and pain is liberating. You understand: *No one else has to change in order for my pain or struggles to go away. My ego tells me that others have to change in order for me to feel successful, happy, fulfilled, or whatever, but I know it comes down to how I process everything.*

So do you process it through the lower identity of your ego and your self-absorption, which allows you to be offended because other people aren't the way you are? Or do you do it through your higher self, which wants you to have peace, feel no turmoil, and experience love?

This is an intelligent system that we are part of; there's an intelligence flowing through us all. Even though it's invisible, you can't get hold of it, and it's impervious to the senses, you just know that this is who you are. You know that you are not your packaging. You can't weigh your life; it doesn't have any form, substance, boundaries, or dimensions beyond the senses. It's beyond the physical— it's metaphysical.

·◇·

You have reached the point where you know you are that which is changeless and eternal, rather than that which is always changing and shifting. You've learned to stand up to your desires. You won't be repressed . . . you're going to be free.

When you live in the light, you experience a sense of peace and bliss, an absence of turmoil. It's really all about love. And when you experience this kind of love, fabulous things happen all the time.

DAILY PRACTICES

Finally, I'd like to offer you a series of suggestions, specific things that you can do on a daily basis to help you enjoy the totally awake, aware, and enlightened life:

— **Remind yourself that you are here to fulfill a Divine heroic mission.** Attempt to serve others in some small way, and do it without telling anyone or looking for any credit. Let go of your own self, and simply ask, "How may I serve others?" Keep in mind that it is in the serving of others that we feel the God within.

Think of some positive, loving thing that you can do without asking for anything back. Practice it sometime today, even if it's just letting someone go ahead of you in line at the grocery store, smiling at those you come across throughout your day, or giving a few dollars to someone in need. Sharing with your fellow human beings brings a sense of joy to everyone involved.

Here is a quotation that I read every single day: "When you seek happiness for yourself, it will always elude you. When you seek happiness for others, you will find it yourself." Remember that the secret of happiness is to stop looking for it yourself and instead try to find it for others.

— **Have a clear picture of something that you would like to see materialize in your life.** Maybe it's attracting the perfect job, finding your soul mate, or achieving optimal health—whatever it may be, keep your inner focus on this picture, and extend love outward as frequently as possible with it in mind. The details will get handled if you can keep the picture in your mind with a knowing; just put love around that picture and don't doubt it. Understand the importance of training your mind, and be sure to have the willingness to do whatever it takes to bring that image into form. Even if you don't see it manifesting for yourself right away, keep the picture there. Before long, you will see what you've been envisioning showing up in your life in the most amazing ways.

— **Have conversations with God in a private and special way.** In these conversations, rather than soliciting favors, affirm your willingness to use all that you are to create solutions. Ask for the inner strength to accomplish something, and then be willing to do what is necessary to make it happen.

As you create this new relationship with the higher part of yourself, you'll see that the strength is there because that's where you place your attention. Remember, where you place your attention is what you're going to create.

— **Remove the concept of "enemy" from your thoughts completely.** The whole idea that there are people on the planet that are our enemies is what the ego has trained us to believe. We have some of these ancient enmities, hatreds, and angers being passed down from generation to generation just on the basis of having whole new souls who come through being taught that "this is whom you're supposed to hate."

Remember, there are no choosing up sides on our own planet. We are all in this thing together. The idea that somehow there are some people who are more special than others is the ego talking again. It's that whole idea of separateness and specialness. Once you have that awareness, the ego is now subsided—you have tamed the ego when you have accepted that there are no enemies.

In my speeches over the years, I've often asked, "How many people are there in Russia?" The audience will give me an answer. Then I'll ask, "Can you think of anybody in Russia whom you hate? Is there anybody in this room who hates someone in Russia? Is there some grandmother over there or one of those little Russian children whom you hate?" There's never a hand that goes up. Yet during the whole Cold War period, we spent billions of dollars creating weapons to kill those very people over there whom no one hates.

The problem isn't so much that we hate others; it's that we haven't learned to love them enough. Once we've learned to love each other enough and completely transcend that idea of having enemies—and when enough of us do it—then we will create peace and foster enlightenment all over the world. We can do that not only with people who are living on the other side of the globe but also with the folks in our own neighborhoods, workplaces, and families. When we can send love to them rather than hatred, we open up the internal energy source that gives us heightened spiritual awareness.

— **Surrender, which involves an act of the heart.** Surrendering takes place in a moment, and the way you do it is by no longer asking, "Why me? Why is this happening to me?" Surrendering means that you simply let go.

When I surrender, I say, "I'm on purpose; I'm only here to serve." I then find that I'm not alone. When you learn to surrender and let go, and realize that you're not in fact alone, you'll have gotten your ego out of the way. The universe handles the details, your higher self begins to rule, and it is bliss.

— **Give yourself time each day for silence.** You can call it meditation, prayer, chanting, or whatever, but give yourself some time each day to get quiet and come to know the voice of God. It isn't so much what you do while you are silent; it's what you are able to bring back from your silence.

If you have something that is really troubling you or you're struggling with, give yourself 20 to 30 minutes to push all the thoughts out. You're going to be able to bring back from that silence the solutions to the things that are such a challenge for you.

The greatest tribute you can give yourself is a moment of silence. Much like when someone passes on who is very dear to us, we give them that moment of silence. Give yourself the same tribute, and you'll find yourself reaching higher states of awareness. This is perhaps one of the most important suggestions I can give you.

— **Lighten your load.** Go through all of the possessions that you no longer use, and share them with others. You can do this with virtually everything you own. Do it both to be charitable and to ease your load. Just lighten up a little bit, and don't tell yourself that you must have these things. Whatever you feel you need owns you, and you can't be enlightened when you are owned by a bunch of stuff.

— **Direct your attention to that which pleases you.** Remember that what you think about is what expands, so keep your mental energy on that which is pleasing and inspiring. Every time you have a thought that doesn't fill the bill, very gently move it out to say, "Next." Pass that one along and keep your attention focused on something higher.

Instead of putting on the television and listening to all of the distressing news and seeking out the kinds of things that only serve to bring you down, put on some gentle music. Try to get out of the habit of having your attention distracted with negativity, which is what the media is really pushing on us today. Surround yourself with positivity—be it by putting on uplifting music or audio programs or just focusing on your empowering thoughts—and you'll see heightened awareness showing up in your life each and every day.

As you continue along your individual process of awakening, can you look back on the "dream" you've been living so far? The ego may try to convince you that you can't really change, that things are the way they are and that's that. When you hear those messages, remind yourself that whatever universal law that has ever allowed any miracle to transpire in the history of humanity, that law has never been repealed. It's still on the books, and it is an energy that is always available to you.

The ego also insists that the world of form is where you belong, this is your place, this is home. Your higher self knows that this is just a transitory stop, for who you truly are is eternal, formless, and changeless, and could never be contained here. You can, however, enjoy heaven on earth, and it's all courtesy of your higher self.

ABOUT THE AUTHOR

Affectionately called the "father of motivation" by his fans, **Dr. Wayne W. Dyer** was an internationally renowned author, speaker, and pioneer in the field of self-development. Over the four decades of his career, he wrote more than 40 books (21 of which became *New York Times* bestsellers), created numerous audio programs and videos, and appeared on thousands of television and radio shows. His books *Manifest Your Destiny, Wisdom of the Ages, There's a Spiritual Solution to Every Problem,* and the *New York Times* bestsellers *10 Secrets for Success and Inner Peace, The Power of Intention, Inspiration, Change Your Thoughts—Change Your Life, Excuses Begone!, Wishes Fulfilled,* and *I Can See Clearly Now* were all featured as National Public Television specials.

Wayne held a doctorate in educational counseling from Wayne State University, had been an associate professor at St. John's University in New York, and honored a lifetime commitment to learning and finding the Higher Self. In 2015, he left his body, returning to Infinite Source to embark on his next adventure.

Website: www.DrWayneDyer.com

Hay House Titles
of Additional Interest

YOU CAN HEAL YOUR LIFE, the movie,
starring Louise Hay & Friends
(available as a 1-DVD program, an expanded 2-DVD set,
and an online streaming video)
Learn more at www.hayhouse.com/louise-movie

THE SHIFT, the movie,
starring Dr. Wayne W. Dyer
(available as a 1-DVD program, an expanded 2-DVD set,
and an online streaming video)
Learn more at www.hayhouse.com/the-shift-movie

·◇·

*The Course in Miracles Experiment: A Starter Kit for Rewiring
Your Mind (and Therefore the World)* by Pam Grout

*High Performance Habits: How Extraordinary People
Become That Way* by Brendon Burchard

*No Endings, Only Beginnings: A Doctor's Notes on Living,
Loving, and Learning Who You Are* by Bernie S. Siegel, M.D.

*The Universe Always Has a Plan: The 10 Golden Rules
of Letting Go* by Matt Kahn

All of the above are available at your local bookstore,
or may be ordered by contacting Hay House (see next page).

·◇·

We hope you enjoyed this Hay House book. If you'd like to receive our online catalog featuring additional information on Hay House books and products, or if you'd like to find out more about the Hay Foundation, please contact:

Hay House, Inc., P.O. Box 5100, Carlsbad, CA 92018-5100
(760) 431-7695 or (800) 654-5126
(760) 431-6948 (fax) or (800) 650-5115 (fax)
www.hayhouse.com® • www.hayfoundation.org

———

Published in Australia by: Hay House Australia Pty. Ltd.,
18/36 Ralph St., Alexandria NSW 2015
Phone: 612-9669-4299 • *Fax:* 612-9669-4144
www.hayhouse.com.au

Published in the United Kingdom by: Hay House UK, Ltd.,
The Sixth Floor, Watson House, 54 Baker Street, London W1U 7BU
Phone: +44 (0)20 3927 7290 • *Fax:* +44 (0)20 3927 7291
www.hayhouse.co.uk

Published in India by: Hay House Publishers India,
Muskaan Complex, Plot No. 3, B-2, Vasant Kunj, New Delhi 110 070
Phone: 91-11-4176-1620 • *Fax:* 91-11-4176-1630
www.hayhouse.co.in

———

<u>Access New Knowledge.</u>
<u>Anytime. Anywhere.</u>

Learn and evolve at your own pace
with the world's leading experts.

www.hayhouseU.com